weren't going to buy it ☺

Thank you for your
friendship and all of our
great talks and planning
Enjoy!

You Don't Have to Worry So Much: Essays

Jeremy McKeen

For Myslik,
whose light and notes I will always look for.

Contents

Acknowledgements

With love and thanks to:

Tanya, Harrison, Zelda, and Tova, all for the first time, and again.

Mom and dad, for years of love and support, and then some.

Lisa Hickey, Wilhelm Cortez, Lori Ann Lothian, Rob Watson, and all the great ones at The Good Men Project.

Melissa Drake, Sarah Fader, Laura Sifferman, Jessica Rapisarda, Alison Tedford, Kara Post-Kennedy, and Gretchen Kelly, who I loved partnering with as writers and activists, and who pushed me to share my voice on the interwebs.

My teaching community peers and my many students who have kept me in their hearts, days, and lives these past twenty years (and a special thanks to the second floor English/Spanish wing for not tearing down that poster from which this book gets its name).

All the rest -- the hundred-plus writers I've been able to edit, old and new best friends, any and all readers of these original posts, and you, the reader.

Anyone I left out, unintentionally or not -- you know who you are.

"I hate quotations. Tell me what you know."

~ Ralph Waldo Emerson

Nobody Asked for an Introduction

YOU DON'T HAVE TO WORRY SO MUCH. You just don't.

We think we do, and we worry like it's going to help (and it does in its own way), but notice I said *so much*. It just makes sense.

Originally this was going to be called **Prodigious Orange Machine Garden Party**, a title based on favorite words of humans (and a writers group), and then one day I realized that not everyone would pick up a book with that title (or would they?!—oh no I've made a horrible mistake!). Another title presented itself in that when I put up a poster at work that just said YOU DON'T HAVE TO WORRY SO MUCH, no one defaced it or took it down for an entire year. An *entire* year. I knew I was onto something. This is a near-impossible task where I work -- high school -- in that nothing ever lasts that long on walls or doors. Students and teacher either liked the sentiment or respected it enough to leave it be. I had a hit title on my hands.

Then came the book. Sort of.

Some chronological notes:
- In 1979, during a blizzard, I was born two weeks late, and I've been catching up ever since. I would later stay an only child, a defining point in my existential and creative acreage.
- In 2011, I finalized my first screenplay and had it bound as part of my graduate fees. This screenplay currently

sits somewhere in my office, collecting lament that I haven't published more of my fictional work, including my first novel, which is still unfinished. I have buckets of fiction to publish someday, and becoming a non-fiction writer was never in my plans.

- In 2012, after years of writing privately in and out of school and grad school, and after many self-aware moments of "knowing" that I am a writer, I started a blog about being a professional human dad and I called it *Nerdy Dad Shirt*. That is where many of these essays started. And yes, they're essays. I teach this stuff for a living, and even though we live in a TL;DR buzzpop fingerful of words world, an *essai* is an essay is an essay. An article is something else.

- Somehow, somewhere in the years that followed, and with thanks to strangers who pushed me online to publish my blog essays on real blog sites, I became part of The Good Men Project as a columnist, which is one of the greatest achievements of my life.

- On the Ides of March, 2015, I hit my head so hard on the frame of our 2005 Saturn VUE that I irreparably damaged my whole life, brain-wise. I now have a disease called Chronic Migraine, and somehow my writing career took off somewhere around the same time.

- In April 2015, The Good Men Project offered me an Editor-at-Large position, a title which I had muscled for, because it wasn't really a thing. They were kind enough to bless me with the title, and there I worked for the next few years, where I got to know the most amazing writers and editors, and was able to be an editor and friend to so many. With this came the privilege of inheriting writers, many of whom I follow with great interest because of their talent, capability, and prodigious strength at the writing game, some of whom are named in my Thanks and Love page.

- All of this was to avoid finishing my novel, *Redbeard in Gypsyland*, which I still haven't finished, which is the reason I'm doing this book of essays because, damnit, I am large and contain multitudes. But this book version is hells better than any blog, and longer than the original essays. And yes, I am furiously finishing that damn novel, which hopefully will be the next thing you'll read, and be like "oh, this prose is so different than that Worry book."

Next time you see "3 minute read" on an article you're not sure you want to read, remember this intro. People need short stuff. We're busy, damn it!

Who reads essays in real life? Hopefully you, for a while. Because here they are.

Enjoy.

-Jeremy McKeen, April 2020

If You've Read This Far, You Win[1]

IF ONLY IT WAS AS SIMPLE as I make it out to be to my high school English students:

- write something effective, brilliant, worth consuming, and the audiences will come running.

Running.

The reality is that no one, aside from me and possibly their moms or tutors will ever read their essay on *Romeo and Juliet* or *Slaughterhouse-Five*.

No one.

The same goes for your blog and your latest I-worked-five-days-and-30-goddamn-hours-on-this-essay or "article" that won't do as well as the random "post" about some human foible/sex angle/sex content/love content that is or has a video and picture to garner 3 million views *and* its own feature on the local news (because the local news takes the run-off from the national news, which could very well feature this bite-size foible and make someone famous for a day as the hosts vamp like they're interested until commercial, then you wait until VH1 calls you for a "Where Are They Now" segment that no one will watch).

Brilliant headline, smart DEK, interesting picture, fingers crossed…

While you slave away on the laptop, *their* piece hits, hits big, *keeps hitting*, and little do they know that often, after the hits subside, nothing happens.

---

[1] *This essay was originally entitled "Read This or My Children Will Starve" or "I Stopped Reading 400 Words Ago (and Other Things You Know the Reader is Doing While You're Working 30 G-D Hours on a Piece that Will Compete with 100,000 Other Pieces for Twelve Seconds of a Reader's Attention Span and Damn It! I Forgot to Put a Number in the Beginning of this Title -- oh Well I'm Sure I'll Have a Hit Next Time)"*

Nothing.

But you're still a writer. You always will be.

If only they could *really* sing, act, dance, build, write comedy, sell products, or write well-rounded essays.

If only.

People get paid for that stuff, you know.

But, thanks to the printing press and cheap ink, anyone with an opinion and enough friends can do anything these days, and the advertisers are licking their chops, ready to sponsor your latest podcast, vlog, or media composite that the world somehow needs right now, right now, and right now.

And, like the images that are produced in volume as street art gain meaning as people see them more and more (but have no intrinsic meaning or talent behind them), these miniature cultural touchstones become our new trading cards, Facebook Likes, and tchotchkes sitting on the shelves of cheaply made cabinets that no one is going to pay full price for at the yard sale.

Most of the material that society is seeing every day (and since time immemorial) is not *50 Essays: A Portable Anthology, America's Best Essays 2016*, or even an essay you'll be forced to read in your ENG101 classes online.

And *that's okay*.

Out of the sea of shares and posts comes new brilliance, literature, nonfiction, and art, and I'm ready for it every time I see it. I really am. It actually excites me to think about it, which is how I know I'm doing the right thing.

After all these years as an English teacher, I still *want to be* an English teacher every day, and the same goes for me as a writer, editor, and reader.

I'm a nut that way. I'm crazy for good art and lit, online or in-hand.

But the Share Culture online—that thing where we're sharing non-stop without really questioning *why* we're sharing—has become our new invented necessity, as has the faux-outrage, faux-sincere-rebuttal, and brilliant listicle posting—as if everything we write should be seen by the world over. #writingnotwriting, #right?

I know that's true for *my* writing, but not everyone else's. Right?

Right?

If you've read this far, you win the internet (and you're obligated to share).

Already you've stopped reading, so I'll close here.

I can feel like you're *about* to share this, but you're waiting for the big reveal or a new twist, and then (and only then) will you post this for someone else to read, to *really, really* read, and there it goes!

So please, pretty please: share this.

Everyone share this.

Share it like you've never shared anything before.

And for my writerly sisters and brothers: be sincere, truthful, and unique in your writing, and make it worthy of the reader—not just because some newfound celebrity depends on it, but because you need to share your truth and story, and we need to read it.

That's it.

It's all and only about the work and the art. That's it.

Because, as an editor and writer, I *need* to keep reading stories from real writers who *can't not write*, as well as from those first-time writers who are still finding their voices.

And if you can't write, and you have something to say, there are plenty of writers out there who will co-write, edit, and ghostwrite your truth for you (not for free, though—and, of course, I'm always for hire).

I will always be reaching, wanting, and helping foster those truths that keep me reading (especially if it is built on real outrage, need, story, anecdote, and controversy), and encourage you to continue doing the same, whether you're the next David Foster Wallace or Big Blog Hit Machine.

Because as long as we've had literature, creative nonfiction, and powerful memoir and bio pieces, we've had yellow journalism, pamphlet sharing, and those extra gospels that just didn't make the final cut but are referenced more than originally intended.

And somehow, after all these years, we're still reading Shakespeare, *Beowulf*, and *The Odyssey* while sharing today's trending topics on our handheld devices.

And that's okay with me.

Even if you stopped reading 400 words ago.

You May Already Be an Old Man

YOU WOKE UP ONE DAY, fully grown, probably in your 30s and with kids, and something about aftershave or toolboxes excited you to your core, and making time to putter around the woodshed, backyard, or basement just made sense. Your metabolism slowed down, and you started seeing the world through slower, more wizened eyes.

What happened?

You got old.

You may actually *be* young, but chances are you're already an old man.

You may have an "old soul" but that doesn't give us the right to call you grandpa, grandpa. What gives us the right is probably your suspenders, or old-as-hell work boots you still think of as "new" when, in reality, you got them fifteen years ago. Or the fact that you think and act like an old man.

Here's how to tell if you're already an old man:

1. **If you're *not* excited about the hardware store, give it time.** Soon you will hear the pulse of Ace or True Value, or even better—a real, hometown hardware store with store credit—calling your name. "Stop by, old man, and buy something," it whispers. "Buy everything here, there's room in the basement for it, and the wife will understand," it says gently, while ushering you to buy more hammers or shovels or a new knife. "Start a new project, you can probably teach yourself from a book," it corrals you.

2. **Are you wearing khakis? You're wearing khakis right now, aren't you, old man?** Yes, you are. You will always wear khakis when you're old. Jeans have lost their youthful touch. Khakis—embrace them, with their crease and endless endurance against all

seasons. Hike them up, and belt them secure enough for a day raking leaves or reading a book quietly. And like jeans, they go with everything, especially work boots—your old, dependable work boots. And a plaid shirt. And a Carhartt jacket. You'll be wearing this uniform until you're dead.

3. **It's 4:30 a.m. and you're awake.** You're just awake. Why isn't everyone else awake? No, no—you need some alone time—all old men do. And you don't have to be at work for a few hours. Maybe the hardware store is open. Or the diner.

4. **Smell that?** That's the aroma of a twenty-minute bowel movement, coffee, and a burnt match. You made that happen, old man.

5. **What time does the diner open? Oh, it's open 24 hours? Well, who goes to a diner at night?** Ok, let's go to the diner, it's almost 6 a.m. Hey, let's do this more often. There are even young waitresses there who put up with your jokes. You're theirs for life now, old man.

6. **If you haven't gone deaf yet, you're starting to, old man.** Friends and family will understand. Just say you're sorry, or ignore them. Your ears have had a good run.

7. **Tightening toilet seats gives you a sense of accomplishment not met with in the first half of your life.** But now—call the papers! You've saved the house from the wiggly wobble of someone's ass slipping off the seat! You've done it, old man! No one else but you could have figured out how to righty-tighty the bolts while your hand was upside down and your forearm was on the part of the seat where everyone puts the most posterior flesh of their butt cheeks. But you did it.

8. **Your haircut is either short or buzzed.** That's just the way haircuts should be. Long hair is for college students and single men in their 20s. Beards are also acceptable, but somehow you don't mind shaving your face every day of your life, because every day is precious now that you're old.

9. **No matter how old you are, you are still and always horny as hell.** This won't change or let up until you're dead, so there's always that. Sorry, old man. Life is full of suffering.

10. **The mention of Scotch or Whiskey—or Bourbon or even Gin—especially the expensive stuff—gets you a little excited.** The more adjectives or descriptors of said liquor, the more excited you get. *Rye whiskey, single-malt…*mention of these things makes you glad you're still alive at your old age. And watching *Mad Men* excites you to no end as well, just for the reason that they're drinking the whole time. Men wearing suits drinking all the damn time means something to you for some reason.

11. **No matter what the current hairstyle is, it looks stupid.** It just looks stupid. The same goes for any new fashion that has arisen since you last bought fashionable clothes years ago, or whenever clothes just started showing up in your closet (it's because your relatives just started buying you what your old man uniform dictates, and you didn't know it, but you started going along with it because you're old now).

12. **No bands or movies or books are as good as the ones from twenty years ago, or whenever it was you grew up, old man.** You're hearing your favorite band on the classic station, and you're kind of deaf to—well, downright pridefully ignorant—new hits. *And* your

favorite artists have become old, too, only they're somehow thinner and better looking than you.

13. **You feel a kinship with anyone your age unlike any other time in your life.** Life has taught you many a great thing, old man, and you're ready for someone to listen to your advice. You've lived, damn it, and you're ready to give someone a piece of your mind, as soon as you read up on how to install your own ceiling or build a set of stairs.

14. **We know you really want to talk about your new Chevy or Buick or sensible automobile purchase, so go ahead, old man.** You only live to old age once. Oh, it was a hybrid truck? Good job, grandpa. We know you got a deal, and we're proud of you. Nobody gets good deals like you.

15. **For your birthday we always know what to get you.** It's whiskey and plaid shirts, right? And a gift card to Home Depot? Or a new pocket knife?

16. **You're a bit of a hoarder, but it's all in good taste and measure...**because you only keep what you need, or that which has value somewhat. You never know when you'll need three mismatched sets of wrenches or old boots or bungee cords or gloves. Or old khakis. Or shovels. You can never have enough shovels. The hardware store probably has shovels. You're on your way to buy a new shovel now, aren't you old man? **We thought so.**

I Don't Want to Do That Thing All Men Do and Then Say 'I Don't Want to Do That Thing All Men Do'

UPSTAIRS, MY SON IS HUMMING.

I can hear him through the floor, two fans, an air conditioner, and my earplugs.

It's wonderful. I love his hum. At eight years old he is a singer and hummer like me, and his youngest sister, the almost-two-year old, hums and sings too. All the time.

The middle child—she used to hum when she was younger, and now she whistles. She always has to be different. But her whistle is one I look forward to, as it's a personal belief of mine that no one should whistle, ever.

And it's wonderful.

Down the hall, my wife is cleaning up and settling into the night and I'm already—just a bit after dinner—back in here working. Always working. It doesn't really matter what I'm working on—it could be going to work, working at home, it could be the same career work you do at home, or a bunch of jobs we do to make ends meet. I feel like I'm beating the system, working hard, longer, ahead—smarter, faster, all hours.

But the system is really beating me. And then I'm beating myself up trying to justify the means with which I'm trying to beat the system.

- *If I worked harder and longer, I'd be more successful, and fulfill my potential.*
- *I have to do this now or I'll regret passing it by, and in the future I'll look back and shake my head.*

- *If I just shaved off some time here and there, I'd be done with the [fill in the blank], and I could finally [fill in the blank].*
- *If I just commit to one more thing, it will be the thing that gets me to the place that I'm supposed to be.*
- *If they just paid me what I was worth, then we'd be all set.*
- *If we could live on less, then we'd be all set (but we're already living on the least of a few options of "the least").*

Thoreau would be so disappointed. Shakespeare too. I've learned nothing, they would tell me, from Hemingway or Miller or Updike or Baldwin. I know of every moral lesson and hard-fought cliché, but I'm trying to "let matter that which matters" and all that.

Self-help writers would be so disappointed—I *should* know better, and I *do* know better, but I can't resist the life that eats up men and makes those self-help writers millions. I'm not making millions. In fact, at my rate, if I saved every penny for twenty years, I *might* have a million.

Inspirational speakers, wizened old leaders, sages of old, preachers, faith-healers, teachers, sagacious grandmothers, hoary seers of ages past, professors, movie producers, poets, grad students—they would all tell me and you and everyone the same. We all know the routine here.

Here's the lesson we're always learning since time immemorial, since *It's A Wonderful Life,* "Cats in the Cradle," every book written about men who work too much, and every film about family being more important than x, y, and z (*work* always being x, y, and usually z): where's daddy? When's daddy coming home?

But I'm doing the thing that all men do and then say I don't really want to live like this.

But we do.

We want to be successful, and fulfill our potential, and have it all. It really isn't that much to ask.

Except that we're all working hard and are broke, just as hard.

We're all living in the lap of First World luxury and beating ourselves up to get more luxury.

And everywhere men are doing it, so much so that I think about the statistics for men and exhaustion, heart attack, and suicide, and how exhaustion, heart attack, and suicide make perfect sense for how we either avoid these pressures or let them build to a consequence that causes us time to pause.

And rest.

And take more time to consider things like family, home, and rest.

But what if?

What if I die without having fulfilled my true and lasting purpose?

What if I get old and miss the chances I could have had, that are right here, right now, but I couldn't see them?

What if being a good husband and father means nothing because the money runs out?

What if—and here's the theme and conflict for the ages—all this is for nothing?

Well, I'm still hopeful. Always holding out for the best. I have to be, right? Considering all other alternatives?

I've been self-aware and examining my life since the notion to do so was novel and I was young enough *not* to be self-aware or have anything worth examining yet.

But even though Shakespeare warned us about the cycle of ambition and what it would get us, and even though the Preacher of Ecclesiastes and generations of nihilists and cynics have doubled-down on the "so what" response to the burning pressure of life, and even though I can quote every line of *Fight Club, Glengarry Glenn Ross,* and *Death of a Salesman,* and despite the fact that Odysseus' journey and heroism is mythical nonsense in that thousands died to bring his name to legend, we all still want it.

We want to be *so alive*, and have it all.

We have it all, and we want more.

We get more, and we want the next thing.

But there's only one Odysseus. And none of us are him.

And as much as I want to—and currently am—fulfilling my potential as a worker, husband, father, and person, I know that you can only fill a cup with so much.

I don't want ex-wives and distant children like the "greats" of each genre.

I don't want a 14-hour-day edging on 16-hours, edging on *never* resting just so I can say I did it my way.

And I'm too old to be Bob Dylan.

But—if I sit still, I can hear my children and wife, and see my life with them, and see my accomplishments so far, and I can be satisfied in this moment, right here, right now.

And that can be enough for a spirit within us that always wants the next thing.

Because it *needs* to be enough, for now, for the ages, for the fit and fever that wants to claim us.

And I don't want to be the voice saying the thing that all men say about the force that drives us to do "the thing" that all men do.

At least not for the moment. When I can be at peace with all the life that is mine up the stairs and down the hall, and in my very self.

And then I settle into the night, and rest for a bit before the next day of things that make us weary and wish for the very chance to be myself and to be alive.

Why God Isn't a Bad Word (It's Just One We Don't Use)

"**MILLIONS OF GODS?** WHAT? Oh my God!" my son exclaimed, appropriately and with emphasis.

I was only a part of the way through teaching my seven-year-old son and five-year-old daughter about what people think a god is, and why my wife and I don't like it when they say "Oh My God."

I was at the part where I explained that there were thousands of religions and millions of gods that people believed in. 330 million-plus gods, to be exact. To be honest, his reaction of "Oh My God" was the most appropriate one I've ever heard, much like when people mean it, which is usually never unless they're in grief or prayer.

This was much easier when I was growing up—before my unbelief took over my reasoning matrix and made me a skeptic and nontheist, back when I was attending church several times a week and getting "saved" every chance I could.

You know, the good old days.

No, your kids aren't going to Hell—they're just not.

Going religion-free after being raised a very specific type of religionist, the question remained: how would we raise our kids? Both my wife and I had similar upbringings, and now we are decidedly nonreligious and comfortable being so to the point of actively raising our kids without the pressure of personal belief, which is a luxury we never had.

So how do you convey the concept of what a god *is* to children without telling them to believe in Gods, and at the same time *not* telling them Gods are all make-believe (even if that's how you really feel)?

If they know that dad and mom *don't* believe in any Gods, and we're telling them that they can or should, then how fair is that to them?

We've waited to tell and teach them about the idea of God because, well, we live Gods-free: my kids know how to be good, where we came from as humans and animals, that monsters aren't real, and that nobody loves them more than we do.

Myth, superstition, and religion go against all of that!

We've already talked about death and feelings and just about everything you can and should talk to children about—they know that you never really die because you live forever in people's hearts and memories even though you can't *physically* be with the person and yes, that makes us sad. And that death is when the brain and heart stop working—and that's it.

No flowery notions of heaven or angels or rainbow bridges. So far we've raised them not to travel mentally to fairy tales when talking about real life things (they do that enough on their own). They both know all about Disney-type magic, myths, and the Force and all the fairy tale kid-things they will grow out of, much like their milk teeth and, for most, religious belief.

They also know about gravity, electricity, physics, and natural selection, to a degree.

How can you be afraid of a thing that isn't there?

But I'm also not afraid of the God talk either. When I was my children's age I was already "born again" and had years (yes, years!) of Sunday school, Bible study, Youth Group, and church packed inside my little kid brain.

By five years old I was "saved," which meant that I had repented of my ugly sins and was a new creature in Christ, and by fourteen I had all the answers I thought I needed, for life. I would go on to evangelize as much as I could to friends, strangers, and all types in-between until, at eighteen, I was on my way to becoming a pastor.

By nineteen I had given up the *belief* ghost because somewhere along the way, God disappeared; God broke up with me; God stopped coming around to the neighborhood of my heart. There *was* no God anymore, and so that was what I pursued, and what made sense, and what was most comfortable.

I tried to get Him back—asking, seeking, knocking—a process taking over the next few years, but there was an empty canvas where there used to be a very detailed painting. I realized that I had acted my way through those years of faith, never realizing (until it was too late) that there wasn't ever anything there except a need to please my family and community, and a sense of a higher reality that promised all the right things.

Why not just be agnostic?

Now that my children are old enough to understand heavier concepts, I talk with them about everything they have questions about, no matter how awkward. But God and religion are specialties for my wife and me, and because our families and country-at-large are so infused with the passion and conviction of personal belief, it's a topic that will never get old, die, or retire.

Plus my kids are amazingly smart and funny, so our talks go in strange directions.

"God is my imaginary friend, and built Fifi (one of her imaginary sisters) the same way he built Jesus," my daughter said after my wife and I explained the idea of Christmas after dinner one night. At six years old, she takes her cues from her brother and parents, so sometimes she *does* believe in God, and sometimes she doesn't. At this point, it's just something extra we talk about.

"Dad, what's the Bible?" my son blurted out in the middle of Thanksgiving dinner, among relatives who have spent good money on Children's Bibles over the years (which, at times, we've read together). This was after he started talking—again—during the prayer, which we had prepared them both for. My answer was a bit sterile, as I was hoping no one heard me or would follow up with criticism or a question.

Everyone heard me, however. We'll see what kind of new Bibles they get for Christmas.

Make-believe on top of make-believe—just cut out the word already.

If you tell a kid there's a magical, invisible force in the sky and all around us who you can talk to every day and who has rules that you have to follow, then you have to follow that up with some sort of reality, like why does that magical force ignore us but love us? And why can't we see that magical force? And then from there you have to literally make up *all* the answers for the kids, which is just more make-believe.

In daily speech if you're *really* thanking God, or calling upon God in prayer (OMG! hear my call!), or calling upon God to damn something, then you're taking the word seriously, which I try never to do, although culturally it seems like we've all been tricked into OMG-ing everything. It's like the "Under God" phrase in the "Pledge of Allegiance" debate: if God was precious to you, why would you want to make the phrase a thing people are forced to say, making the special nature of the phrase become boring? Or why would you want to put God's precious name on money?

Using *God* incorrectly seems as bad as not using it at all, which I just happen to do on a daily basis.

Like I have explained to my kids: when talking, you don't have to say anything at all when bad, tumultuous, good, or surprising things happen, just to show your emotion. *"Oh wow"* or *"ay de mi"* or *"oy vey"* works just fine—or "Oh my Ghoul" as the *Monster High* girls say.

Words are the most powerful tools we have, so use them wisely.

My *unbelief* is just as powerful as anyone's active belief, and just as important.

As they grow, my children are going to believe or act the way they truly feel guided to believe or act, and hopefully they won't do anything in life just because they want to make my wife or me happy. I won't ever be dishonest with them about the things that matter most to us, or how we see things that matter most to other people who we love (who might see things differently).

As a writer, teacher, and parent, I know the importance of words in life and culture, especially since little ears are always listening, and ready to ask a follow-up question.

Especially during a family meal, when all the siblings and parents (but still, just those at the table) are listening.

Just Don't Be a Shitty Dad

DADS: **STOP HIDING IN THE BATHROOM,** garage, shed, backyard, bar, and at work.

The kids and wife will find you there eventually.

It's okay, all you have to do is play with your kids, be nice to your wife, and give them your entire mortal life and all the attention, beauty, and care inside it. That's all.

There are secrets to a long, beautiful life, and one day, when the kids are out of the house, you will have the bathroom *all* to yourself (between their college years and your death) and you'll miss being interrupted all the time with urgent matters like who hit who, who is bothering who, who needs to really, really, *really* go to the bathroom right now (so it's *not* okay to have the kids pee in the tub while you're occupying the throne?).

If you're reading this *and* you're a dad, you're probably not needing the "advice" I'm going to shell out. But most people out there can be shitty, awful people, and especially to their kids. But if, by chance, an awful human being has become a parent, I'm hoping he would somehow stumble upon this essay. *Somehow.*

So chances are you're *not* a shitty dad. Maybe you're a first time dad or finally reconnecting with your kids after some estrangement. No judgment here. It's almost never too late to raise your children right.

But if you *were* tending toward that reality, here are some pointers to pass along.

Be there. Just be there.

Absenteeism by dads is an epidemic in America and the world. There is no greater struggle, archetype, or therapy-prompt than "talk about your relationship with your dad." By just being there all the time you've saved a future broken human being from suffering from thoughts of insecurity and abandonment at their current and future age. Fight hard against the struggles and obstacles of life to be there for every moment you can, even if it seems like they don't want or need you there.

Don't be a selfish asshole with your time.

Your *stuff* isn't that important. The kids want your attention, and if you don't give it to them, they will get the hint and not bother you again, or they'll give their attention to *anyone* else, preferably not you--maybe for life. But don't helicopter over them all the time either. Everyone needs some time alone sometimes, but not *that* much time. One day you're going to get home late and realize you haven't talked to your kids in a few days, and you'll wonder where all the hours went. Play this scene over in your mind and adjust accordingly. This also goes for your precious stuff that you don't want them touching.

Just play princess or LEGOs or whatever with your kids. Just do it.

Whatever you're doing is not as important as tea party, princess ball, picnic, kitchen, school, construction site, or any of the wonderful games you could be playing with your amazing, perfect children. Whatever they're into, they're looking for reinforcement and approval. Play all the games they want, and engage them on their level as much as you can before they fade out and revert to only playing by themselves. You are the most important person in the world to them, for now.

Turn off the TV after a little bit, or for good.

Remember Jim Carrey's character in *The Cable Guy* plummeting to his death? His last words were, "Kill the Babysitter," referring to the boob tube that had "raised" him.

This goes for YouTube, handheld devices, and tablets. Kids should be experiencing plenty of fresh air, free play, and whatever it is you're doing away from the couch. Whatever you're doing, include them, even if it's "above their heads" (which will probably never be the case unless you're splitting the atom or doing advanced grammar or calculus–even then, that's pretty cool to share). Once the television and smartphone are off, you can actually *feel* the parasites leaving your brain to go onto more creative uses of your time with the kids.

Learn with your kids.
Kids are crazy sponges and love to explore and learn. So expose them to all the not-so-boring things you want to learn, and be pleasantly surprised when they take it as seriously as you. They are literally blank slates, so fill up their brains with great life stuff. This also goes for all your favorite music and hobbies. Your kids want to learn what you like, because they really, really like you and all the things that make you, you. For now.

Talk a lot and use big words.
Successful adult humans often have strong educational backgrounds because of their parents' education and willingness to share words and ideas. It's not too late or too early to get all the knowledge in your head into theirs. You are your child's first teacher, so have something good to say, and don't water down your vocabulary. And read to them and with them, and make sure they see you reading.

Don't hit your kids.
Getting a "switch from the tree" or "bopping" your two-year old just isn't necessary. Time outs, taking away privileges, and a loud, mean voice of authority often work just as well. "Spoiling the child by sparing the rod" makes no sense when you consider that *hitting your kid with a rod* would be awful. A

grown man hitting a little kid because he spilled his juice or did something naughty has no correlation in the real world unless you're equating violence in prisons with people actually *learning* something about life, which isn't happening. Most people hit their kids between ages 2-12 and then *don't* hit anymore when the kids get older (although we all know the hitting can continue long after 12 or until the child is big enough to hit back). Doesn't that seem illogical? At the most precious memory and skill-forming time in the child's life, you're using physical aggression and violence to teach important lessons? They can't learn any other way? I think–and know–not.

Just be yourself, or the better version of yourself you hope to be.

Your kids are going to solidify an image and character of you and stick with that for life, so give your best to them, always. Don't worry about being perfect, and don't be afraid to learn from new mistakes. You can reinvent yourself as you learn how to parent, and start taking your kids on all the adventures you've been putting off until you thought life would somehow magically open and encourage you to start *really* living. It did open up: you had kids. You created human life and it can talk, walk, and think just like you did all those years ago. There's something powerful in that.

When all else fails, just say to yourself, *Just don't be a shitty dad.*

You can be a shitty spouse or son, worker or friend, brother or citizen, but just don't shortchange your children, ever. At your funeral let the living say that you were the best father you could have been, you loved your kids, and gave them the world and then some. Whatever that means to you, apply it and stick with it, and enjoy your kids while you can. Tell them you love them at least a thousand and one times a day, and show them that you love them that many times and more. They'll love it. Because all they want is you.

Do the Thing You're Doing -- How to Say Yes to Your Full Potential

JUST DO THE THING YOU'RE DOING. Right now. I'll wait.

I'm serious. Just do one thing for the next several moments.

Done? Okay, good. Let's talk.

If you're like me, your brain looks like -- and you feel like -- a sped-up train station, with all trains, people, vendors, workers, and the rails themselves needing attention all the time, and all at the same time, right this minute. You're working in the top tiers of Maslow's Hierarchy, but your work and parenting time, or your work and "be a real person" time all blend together until you escape the trainyard of the moment, breathe, and then return to working some more.

At some point, time disappeared and the whole calendar felt like it was always happening, all the time. While busy at work, you're really busy with issues from home, or using work time for personal things you can't get to any other time, and all the while you feel the eternal speed-demoning inside your heart, as if you don't get this done right now, it'll be the end.

It won't be the end, will it?

During this type of non-stop rat race, you think that everything you're doing is leading to something better or some idealized moment, and, you think, the future is just waiting for you to arrive—road-weary, sick, tired, beat up, but ready for glory.

Why do we think this way? What's so wrong with the present moment that we're always trying to avoid it?

It can be a Catch-22, right in the chest.

There I was, back flat on the table for an EKG after complaining about chest discomfort, chatting with the nurse about what causes nondescript chest pain—again. This was my umpteenth time in the E.R. or doctor's office for this kind of worrisome nonsense since my early twenties.

"Anxiety," she said, knowingly, although she wasn't "supposed" to say anything. She knew and I knew, and during this particular visit I was in an actual hurry to see the doctor because of the tired, old cliché that "I just don't have time to be sick" or "I can't afford to take time off work to see the doctor."

I had to be somewhere. I always have to be somewhere.

"Nondescript chest pain" usually means you're too young to have that heart attack (you know, the one you're waiting for so you can finally take some time off to relax) but you're too stressed to let the muscles around your heart and in your back relax as well.

So at some point I had to get smart, and, while at work the week after, as I was racing from one task to the next, I stopped in my tracks and wrote a note to myself:

Just do the thing you're doing, right now.

When I first wrote it, I thought of the profundity of it, and, like all good advice, I smiled and then ignored it.

But then I thought—what if I really did this? I mean, I already try to do this with my own children, students, and athletes. My whole philosophy of life is built on "being here now" and yet I'm often looking toward the day or week to end so I can breathe.

So from this one idea, I had to remind myself of the other aphorisms I've forgotten along the way, like:

Say no to something each day—Or better yet, pick something each day not to worry about.

Don't take on something new without giving something else up first—if all the things you're currently doing aren't so cumulatively great that you would trade more of your time for new ventures that could eventually push out the original ventures, then what is the point of all the things you're doing?

(And still, even while I'm writing this to you about not doing everything at once, my brain is planning several other things.)

Stop thinking that the next thing is going to complete you.

It might, but it won't. It's not. Well, maybe it is. Will it? Oh shit. Wait. How do I know it won't?

If you're not "complete" right now, at your age, with your life choices and direction, then chances are that just doing more or taking on a new position or title won't complete you right away. If something seems too good to pass up, it might just be too good to be true.

So take your time, even if it's sped-up-train-station time.

Settle into the moment—and force yourself to settle if you have to.

Be selfish with your down time, if you get any. If you don't get any, make some. Eventually your body is going to make you rest, if you don't. You know, the whole stress thing—the poor choices you make while being rushed all the time will catch up to you and you'll be sick, tired, and a day behind when you can't afford a day to be behind on.

Plus you need the perspective of stopping, breathing, and looking at everything around you.

Get by with a little help from your friends (and spouse, and family).

Don't be a dead hero to everyone because you couldn't accept help from those people in your life who you're actually working for and working with. Ask for help, whatever it is— the minute you do, a stream of bright light will shoot forth from your head and open up the realm of possibilities to you and the world based on the fact that you're a mortal who can't do everything yourself.

Did you already know that?

The kids—whatever you're avoiding the kids for, give it a break.

They want you around. They want your undivided attention. When they get tired of you and want to be by themselves or play and read on their own, let them know that you need some time as well. But don't ever avoid them because they're in the way. They are the way. They're the whole way and the work that leads to the way.

And one day they won't be around so easily, and they will remember every time you couldn't stop being busy to play with them.

The spouse or significant other—make time now. Just do it.

If you're not talking to your significant other about your stress levels or anxiety, why not?

Vices will feel great, but will not solve anything…

Addiction, overindulgence, or vices won't solve your problems, as much as they may give relief for the time being (as much as they force us to relax and be in the moment). They often become stressors unto themselves and most of us drink or use drugs long after the thrill and punch is gone, or our tolerance has risen far above where it was when we started. That's too stressful.

Most of us are already over medicating, overdrinking, overeating, or allowing something to give us temporary relief at the expense of our bodies, when you could just slow down and focus on one thing, like getting a good night's sleep, for example, or eating right. This seems simple, but many of us are in physical pain as well as stressed out from work and family, and can't think straight enough to slow down and just drink a glass of water thoughtfully.

Besides, drugs and alcohol cost money, and money costs time, and you need more time to relax.

Your life is now complete!

So what are you doing—right this moment? Hopefully it's just one thing, like just one thing. If not, take a deep breath, and take a deep moment, and remember why it is that you do what you do. Turn off the television and the smartphone notifications, and listen to the silence, if you can hear it.

It literally will mean everything in the world.

Now where do you have to be?

A Letter to the World on Behalf of Everybody's Child

To be handed out, shared, spread, copied, memorized, and dropped into all countries, for the rest of time immemorial.

TO WHOM IT MAY CONCERN, Which Is Everyone, the World Gone Round, Complete:

I have a child on the way.

She will be the greatest person, entity, and force in the Universe and I want nothing bad to happen to her, ever. I mean scrapes, bruises, and childhood bumps are okay, and the occasional cold and fever will be allowable, but I'm talking about the big, scary, preventable stuff. She will be the latest addition to our family, and the following also applies to my wife, son, and first daughter—who are also the greatest people, entities, and forces in the Universe.

So, to preserve her life against all ills and manners of human-imposed violence and destruction, I need you to take a few things seriously.

First off—and what you need to understand is—I want you to consider that my child is your child, and vice versa.

To take away my child from me would be the worst thing known to humanity. Therefore I want to get rid of this possibility from our life on this world.

Once you understand this, it will eliminate a lot of violent oversight, in that I would never harm your neighborhood or village or state or town or city because I know your child is there, and I wouldn't want to hurt her or her future (this also goes for your child's mother and family and friends, as it would mine).

There is nothing worth destroying your child for—not money or land, not pride or belief, not resources or ideas. Let me just restate this so I'm understood:

There is nothing worth destroying your child for. Nothing.

I would never want to take your life or your child's life for something I need or want to have. That would be foolish and selfish, and wouldn't be something I would want to teach my child. If there is conflict, then we can work it out somehow, whatever it is. We can share, or better yet we can trade and borrow and lend, and hopefully we'll keep it clean and fair and reasonable. Or if we really can't see eye to eye, we can walk away and be friends in the future somehow. I also hear that love and forgiveness are options worth trying. You love your child, and I love mine. We're not that different.

This being stated and understood, there are some big things I think we can work on to eliminate the chance that our children *won't* survive, namely disease and poverty. Poverty often leads to disease, and disease can make the wealthiest become impoverished, so we're really talking about these two. Whatever cures my tribe has to share, I promise to share them with your tribe so that your children will live. And my tribe has a lot to share. Nobody's child should die from easily preventable sickness or hunger, ever. No child should be hungry or sick for any preventable reason. And this is something we can work on and perfect. We have enough tools and time.

That's about it. If we can secure these two points, I'm sure everything else—education, science, technology, medicine, access to resources, music, the arts, et al—will fall into place. If they *don't* fall into place (or fall into something better or different), then hopefully our children will get together and help us see that we are more alike than different, or that we don't have to bicker about it. Or that whatever it is that is separating us might be a meaningless thing, far under the importance of community and providing for the long life of our children. But our children need to be alive, healthy, and free if we're *not* going to heed this advice until the next generation.

To end, dear world, and all the whoms that are in it, I wish you and your children peace and satisfaction.

I may not live in your land or share your customs or gods or traditions, but I know what it is to be a father and a child. By the time my children are grown, hopefully there will be a better, cleaner, safer, and healthier world for their sons and daughters. If not then we will have to try again until success (what and whenever that may be) is achieved.

We, as a race, have been trying this for millennia, and sooner or later we'll get good at it.

In love, hope, and peace,

A Father

7 Ways We Can Save the World (for All Time)

THERE HAS NEVER BEEN A TIME in history better than now to be alive. Really.

If you live in the "First World" of industrialized nations, you can literally be homeless and sick, and be better off than 87 percent of the rest of the world.

Humans worldwide today are healthier, more educated, and living longer than 99 percent of humanity thus far. There are at least 100 billion souls buried in the Earth who never had it this good.

Humanity isn't without its faults, however, and the Earth is far from fixed. So here are seven ways to save the world for the next seven-to-fourteen generations:

1. *Fix Yourself*—The old saying of "if you fix the man, you fix the world" still rings true. Chances are that there are several things you could be working on that you're either avoiding or hoping will go away. You might be letting fear or pride blind you in daily decision-making. You might be living for the wrong principles. You might just need to listen more to your partner, friends, and children who need you. Whatever the case, it only takes one good man to make a positive difference for thousands of others. Be that one.

2. *Save the Children*—Corrupted adults who turn their backs on helping humanity had a start somewhere, and there are millions of neglected children who will grow up without the anchored, centered feelings that a grown person needs to see clearly. Everybody needs a chance in life—especially if that person is a child without a mentor, teacher, coach, or trusted adult.

3. *Be Aware of the Corruption!* —Even the "cleanest" and most moral of us become thieves, cheaters, and killers.

Temptation is everywhere, and unless you are aware of your own nature, it will be hard to resist temptation and vice when the time comes. Be prepared, and prepare yourself to always make the right decision. This is extremely difficult and why the world is the way it is in the first place, right?

4. *Learn How to Wait*—Patience is the key element to succeeding at life, overcoming stress, and being at peace with who you are and who you are transitioning to become. If you learn how to wait your turn, or how to be patient with people who have never been treated with patience, you're going to see a whole new side of life worth living.

5. *Be Good and Good For Something*—This may sound cliche, but we have set up the modern world to run on a system of exploitation and deceit, where we bet money and blood on the lowest common human denominators. You may be good at something that isn't a "good" at all, or part of a system that needs more good people like you to fix it from the inside out. Choose your mission carefully, and be the standard for goodness to those around you.

6. *Run for Office*—Yes, you. Run for something, no matter how small. Your town needs you to make a positive change and to steal daily life back from the crooks (who are everywhere). And don't run because your ego needs a boost or because you think you may be "the one"—but run because if you don't, someone with less of a conscience will, and we've all seen that play out a million times before, since the dawn of time.

7. *Be the Hero You Think Should Exist Where You Are*—Regardless of your work in life, you need to realize that it takes a world of people to provide a better world for people. You may work tirelessly to fight injustice seven days a week, but you can be guaranteed that there is

injustice somewhere happening all the time, and it's not your fault. You can only do so much good. That's why it's important to start where you are, treating the people around you with goodness. That's all you can do. You're only one person, but you may be the first person in a long line of good people to continue the *seemingly* impossible task of saving the world.

So get going, ace! It all starts with you today — there has never been anything different or truer or more daunting than you living your role in daily life, and being good at it while being good for something good.

5 Easy Steps to Staying Married Forever

SOME OF YOU SHOULD NOT BE MARRIED. You know who you are, possibly. It's hard to tell unless you *get* married and then realize, at some point, that it isn't for you—or that it *was* at one point, and is no longer (possibly when you were young and your brain wasn't fully formed), especially when it's supposed to be *forever*. The funny thing about that is that "forever" is a time-sensitive concept for mortals who usually die before their 100s, but the sentiment is nice. If marriage really meant you'd be married forever, even after death, possibly while populating planets for all of eternity, then it might change the conversation.

But that's not marriage, that's a sci-fi concept most people fear.

The idea for couples is supposed to be "until *death* do you part," but it seems that, like most young people who don't know yet that they aren't invincible, death is a far-off concept, and not at all considered by the very ones who should be considering it. So *death*, then. Or, you know, until something better or less boring comes along. Or until the kids are a little older. Or until that final fight to end all fights, and you need someone new.

It's hard not to be cynical about marriage in an age where our heroes and culture constantly celebrate and—at the same time—dismiss the very real and personal choice to enter into wedded bliss.

Most marriages end the same way "best friends forever" relationships end: they were, for a time, relevant. Then something happened, and then the couple realized that their time was up sooner than death or forever. The statistics are enough to make the most hopeful of matchmakers quit their day jobs: marriage is a *crumbly* institution, even on the second and third take, and most married people (up to 70 percent for both genders in some studies) cheat on their spouses at some point. The National Center for Health Statistics and federal studies have shown that "one-third of new marriages among younger people will end in divorce within 10 years and 43 percent within 15 years."

Yikes on bikes built for two.

1. Don't get married. Just don't do it. Unless...

Before you know it, you'll be married and eating pizza and wings on your couch with your beloved, staring at the next seven to eight decades of your life. It's going to happen. But why? It seems that most humans gravitate towards marriage or at least domestic partnership, so we're talking about a deep, human tradition that doesn't have to require a license and rings. But most people spring for the legal side of it, changing last names and throwing a big party with cake and a DJ (or, if they're really good, a house band).

But marriage, while practiced by almost every adult, shouldn't be. This is evident in the divorce rates for first and second-time spouses, which show us that more than 40 percent of us just aren't good at staying married and faithful (if you're the kind of person who wants a faithful spouse). And 90 percent of us won't take on that second marriage until its mortal end.

What we're good at is *getting* married because, well, why not? Contrary to statistics, it makes sense to become domesticated and want to be with someone forever.

2. You must first *like* the person you're marrying

Soon, as a married couple, you will be (or be near) old, fat, balding, and without any of the charm you might have once had. It happens. You're going to live and suffer through life with one person who is supposed to be magically matched to your personality.

So you should like that person.

Yes, love is important. Some would say it's all you need, but they were wrong. You must like the person you're going to suffer through life with. And I use the word "suffer" in all of its meaning, from the light stuff to the heavy: changing jobs, having kids, losing loved ones to death and distance, and the never-ending money problems (if you're alive and have a bank account, then you will have money problems at some point, and sharing a bank account is just as a risky experiment as marriage itself).

So you have to like the person, and want to be with them all the time. Now you can't make yourself like someone, so right here we have one of the reasons divorce is so popular: hordes of *marriers* who just stopped liking the person they pledged their life to.

Before marrying I had a number of girlfriends who I liked and loved. But there was always an indication that I needed to get out of the relationship before I stayed too long at the party. This inner navigation, or "voice" usually spoke to me along the lines of "oh no, you don't like her any more—get out now," and luckily I listened, every time, even when I had played too long.

But with my wife, I never had that voice. I'm in love with my wife, of course. But I really *like* my wife, and that counts for so much more. She and I have built a world that I really like, and look forward to every day of my life. Love is easy. But the hardest thing in the world is to get someone to like something—or someone—they just don't.

3. Don't cheat—Don't fucking do it

Think about this: up until the last hundred years or so (and still, today, in many parts of the world), we've had, over hundreds of thousands of years of human culture and tradition, multiple versions of marriage. From legally bound and slave wives, sister wives, and child brides to polygamy and same-sex marriage, "the institution of marriage" is a prodigiously layered creature.

But in the First World, we've accepted "monogamy until death" as the majoritive and legal norm, and have come up with many variations of cheating as to define the things that draw us away from that one legally bound person.

Whether it's an emotional affair or harmless flirting, the best thing is to a) identify the attractive element that leads you to stray, b) call it what it is, and c) fucking walk away from it. But most people don't and never will do that. In fact, most people seek a secret freedom within their marriage where they hope they will be able to betray their spouse *and* have the best of both worlds. Only one world includes someone who will be made a fool out of, and the other usually ends abruptly or embarrassingly so. And the relief that comes from the end of a cheating relationship is never worth the pain it causes all parties.

But what's so great about both worlds when each is incomplete at some point? Some marriages or committed relationships start with infidelity, and end up lasting. There's no judgment here. There are better ways to end a partnership than humiliating your best friend and then going broke to pay people to legally separate you from the very same old best friend.

4. If it works (and it's healthy), then it works

Some people are so miserable in their marriages and it's not the fault of the marriage or spouse, it is just that certain time period they are stuck in. Those who marry young or marry because of a child on the way, or those who marry because religious doctrine demands it, might just make it and stay married until death. Or not. There's no prescription for how long or how happy a marriage should be, except that it should be healthy and work. Some marriages only work for a few years, and the individuals involved are smart enough to call it quits. Some marriages work here and there, and last decades, even lifetimes. And some people do very well going from relationship to relationship and never marry.

Think about it: more of us in our 30s and 40s are marrying later in life because we've had several relationships that didn't end in marriage, and this taught us what to look for in a first marriage. There shouldn't be any shame in divorce nor should there be in not getting married. Finding someone who works and is healthy for you is the only thing that matters, especially if you're going to have children. But there is no perfect narrative except the one you're working on, and hopefully building with the person who is right—and healthy—for you.

5. There is no fairy tale ending, unless there is

Our way of life, from multimedia storytelling to tabloid culture and news coverage is consumed with pairing—the tragedy and comedy of it, the minutiae of it, and the never-ending lead-up and break-apart of it. It is what fuels us. Kids will come and grow, careers will sprout and break, and we'll still be flirting in the nursing homes and wrap-around decks of our houses in retirement.

The spouse who leaves a marriage for a better life, with or without another spouse, might just create that fairy tale ending. The reality, however, is that the *ending* doesn't last until death. An ending is an *ending*, with a strong rising action, turning point, and years of falling actions and revelations leading up to it. Our problem is that we're too damn young and think life is cemented for us each decade; we should know better now that we're living longer, and look forward to each year as a regrouping of our sensibilities about life and our choices with our spouse.

Most people just want someone who loves and accepts them, and will keep their spot free on the couch after a long day. We want to belong to someone amazing and build a small tribe to carry on that legacy. Or something like that.

And, for the record, if I could stay with my wife forever, even after death, and just host and go to afterlife parties for all of eternity with her as my date, then I'd be just as happy as I am sharing the couch with her after the kids go to bed in the here and now, and on until retirement, and then until my final breath. I really like her, like *like* her. More than all the others in the world.

Mazel Tov!

Why No One Really Believes in the Song "Imagine"

YOU MAY SAY THAT I'M A DREAMER, BUT I'M NOT.

There is rarely a time that I hear the song "Imagine" when I don't get a little choked up and sentimental towards a hopeful world.

The anarchic, atheistic, socialistic, rebellious nature of the song has somehow worked its way into the heart of Americana, where even the most pious of listeners will admit they love the song and that somehow it is definitive of some overarching philosophy we should all belong to.

And I agree, some of the time. Well, most of the time. Well, almost.

As a writer and musician and teacher, I approach the song for what it's worth: a radical look at the fabric of society, and how to create a lowest common denominator so that we can, one day, end war and live in relative or actual peace. But aside from that, it's total nonsense that none of us could actually strive for, although we all think we are.

A few steps toward this understanding:

Nobody Really Believes in Heaven, but yet Almost Everyone Does.

To "Imagine there's no Heaven/It's easy if you try/No hell below us/Above us only sky" is pretty simple unless, like MOST people you've been raised with an idea of Zoroaster's Hell-Heaven dynamic. Most people want bad people to suffer for their crimes and then be rewarded for their own do-good. Even the most lapsed Catholic isn't going to give up her idea of some "Titanic ending"-like Heaven where Leo welcomes her to the party. However! If pressed, people WILL admit that Heaven is a tricky idea, like Santa Claus' system of naughty and nice. And those fundamentalists will be a little shy to tell you that they believe in a stark Hell-Heaven contrast.

Just imagine how hard it is to say "I believe in Heaven and Hell, and you're going to Hell. Now…you wanna hang out?" However! If John wanted us to imagine there was no Judgment, and no Party Hereafter, a lot of people take solace in both, and, well, it does make the glory of War a little sweeter. Just ask the Klingons.

Nobody Really Lives for "Today"

I mean, we like to think we do, but most of us are living a month at a time, or not thinking about living at all. We just do it. Or at least we think that we'll live forever. If not forever, at least until our 70s. And if we did live just for today, that "for today" reality (some hyper-YOLO or Carpe Todayem) would make us do the things that would jeopardize peace tomorrow, like stealing, lying, killing, cheating, and worse parts of self-interest. As humans we still do every entire awful thing anyway, because we're constantly caught between choosing Long-Lasting Satisfaction and Immediate Gratification. (Hint: choose the first in most cases).

Nobody Really Wants No Countries

C'mon Lennon! We LOVE boundaries! We love gangs, parties, families, clans, tribes, and clubs. We love a good town line. As nice as it sounds, people need a sense of geographical identity, unless they're Mennonites. Or from Jersey.

Nobody Really Wants Nothing to Die For

Imagine there is nothing to kill or die for? What? John come on! Humans LOVE to kill, and die for the dumbest shit. Shoes, money, honor. These humans are NEVER going to give up dying for anything. Hell, even you died at the hands of some pudgy asshole for no reason. Oh, wait.

Nobody Really Wants No Religion

330,000,000 million gods and 6,000 religions in the world and people are going to give this up? Religion is a way of life, even for non-theists (what would we argue about?). Even the most lapsed Buddhist is going to say "Buddhist" at the hospital when they ask what religion he is. Maybe not. But if there were no religion, we would be all too quick to create it again. We need purpose to fill up our social hierarchy unless we want to admit that we're just walking protozoa in need of DNA replication and a few giggles before death.

Nobody Really Wants a Brotherhood of Man

They just don't. Not even fraternity brothers or real brothers like each other that much. Imagine if you had 3 billion brothers and 3 billion sisters! The holidays would be awful.

Nobody Really Wants No Possessions

People LOVE their stuff. Even Communists. Even the hippiest of hippies at the most liberal commune loves at least one iota of their "stuff." Even monks begging in the street value their tunic and bowl. This one is too hard, John. Even 18-month-olds are greedy.

Nobody Really Wants a Dreamer

People want cheap food, a couch, and entertainment. And freedom. And hugs. That's pretty much it, John. And Steve Jobs was not a dreamer. He took a TV, typewriter, and computer board and marketed a sandwich, essentially.

Nobody Really Wants To Be "One" With the World

Whatever "one" means you can rest assured that less than 1 out of 10 people would want to suffer with someone else and share the awful existence that goes on in the world. Sure we'd like to share the beauty and wonder of existence, but most people only marry one person at a time. Imagine marrying

ALL the world! Get it? Imagine? People like to be segregated, and think they're better than other people. Hell, I love alone time. United People is still a pipe dream. Even among United People you have terrible class structures. And this song is about destroying all class structures.

Nobody Really Wants...
Ah, Hell. It Is A Great Song. In my heart, I'm with you, John. Now drop the ball, and let's sing along.

5 Brand New Fallacies That Will Let You See Every Argument Clearly (and Win as Well)

FOR YOUR NEXT ARGUMENT, don't just rely on the evidence, the kindness of your debate partner, emotion, or the sound nature of the argument itself—rely on stone cold logic. Or something close to it.

Add these new fallacies to your mental lexicon, and remember to argue with kindness (or else you'll be feeling the brunt of the "Nobody Wants to Hang Out with Him Anymore" fallacy).

You may be familiar with some of the common fallacies like Ad Hominem, Slippery Slope, Circular Reasoning, No True Scotsman, and Argument from Authority. There are many common fallacies and hybrids.

For your arguing pleasure (and in the hopes you aren't the Fool), here are several new fallacies we all keep repeating, whether in debate or daily life:

The YOLO Fallacy
The YOLO fallacy says that whatever you do in honor of a Carpe Diem attitude is justified because you only live once when in fact you only die once (that we know of), you live every day, and life is pretty long. YOLO casualties should be kept to a minimum, because if people really lived like it was their last day alive, then we'd be in an even bigger mess than we already are.

So you have to be careful how you treat people and things, not just once, but all day—every day.

The Big Crush Fallacy
Romantic crushes are called so because of that painful compression you feel when you realize that your crush doesn't

feel the same way—however, the Big Crush Fallacy has to do with the delusion that your crush likes you and is sending you cryptic signals. Avoid the "crush" here: that is, avoid the self-fulfilling prophecy or the want to believe in signs that aren't actually there.

If you believe in something the same way that a person who has a crush on somebody believes that there's a chance for romance with the target of their obsession, you can actually delude yourself into thinking that something is true when it's not. Don't get crushed.

The Recycle, Recycle, Recycle Fallacy

If we just keep recycling things that shouldn't be in the waste stream—and that waste stream could be our veins, homes, and workplaces as well as our waterways—then we're avoiding the fact that some of those things should be cut off at the source. Reduction or elimination should be the real solution. Why do we put up with pollution and poison? Because pollutants don't always start out as pollutants—they can be suggested or agreed-upon solutions at first, and then they amass or dominate the "stream" and we find out their true nature (or that we just can't recycle our way out of it).

If we reduce our intake or stop our consumption (plastic bottles, too much sugar, name your polite vice), then we're actually getting at the root of the problem rather than rehashing the same set of problems that were created in the first place.

Just Keep Injuring People and Things until It All Gets Better

This could also be titled the **War is Peace Fallacy**, which states, incorrectly, that somehow things will get better—magically— if we hurt enough people (and keep hurting, and keep hurting). The results of this common human fallacy are all around us, and sprinkled throughout history (and in every mafia, political thriller, and action movie out there, not to mention current events). It assumes that if we keep injuring, exploiting, using, and murdering people that, at some point, the resolution will present itself and things—for the house, company, or state—will become ideal. This is magical thinking at its worst that the "lesson" that the perpetrators are inflicting will somehow become apparent to all, and all will be well in the end.

I Never Need Help, so I'll Never Need Help

This fallacy's inverse is also true: I always need help, so I'll always need help. Don't be afraid to see that doctor or ask your spouse or friend for an honest opinion. Things change, and there's no shame in needing—or not needing—real, genuine, and lasting help every now and then.

13 Life Lessons from the First Twenty Years of Teaching

AFTER TWENTY YEARS OF TEACHING high school English in the city *and* having my own children in the public schools for a few years now, I'm old enough to have learned something important enough to share, and young enough to realize that I'm looking down the line at twenty-plus more years until I'm too old to keep up with my last senior class, who won't even be born until 2024.

I remember my first taste of teaching when I was a student-teacher. I was 100 percent student and 100 percent teacher, only a few years older than the pupils themselves, my book bag heavy with three years of Education and English classes, and zero classroom experience, lucky to have some great mentor teachers to mold my enthusiasm. I loved it with a specific mixture of expectation and excitement that I still retain. When I get tired of it or stop having fun, I will have to pass on the green correcting pen.

My first year teaching I was twenty-two, and some of my students were nineteen. *Nineteen.* Suffice it to say I had also been a theatre major, so I acted my way to seeming like an older professional. I still got the "hippie teacher" moniker (and I still do), so I chose a genuine track of personality, and found that being myself—and an earnest professional—worked in the smaller moments (and the bigger moments too).

But I'm no longer the younger teacher getting advice from the wizened old curmudgeons recalling the good old days of the 1970s, when lawlessness ruled the hallways and kids left for lunch to get lit at the bar. Now, in my later 30s, *I'm* the old guy with seniority. And by the time I retire, I will have taught, advised, coached, and worked with nearly 10,000 kids.

Here's what I've learned, more or less:

1. There is no such thing as a bad kid.

There just isn't. That first paragraph from *The Great Gatsby* about people not having the same advantages as other people? It applies every day in almost all situations, for the poor and middle and upper class students alike. In an age of awareness and daily treatment of ADD/ADHD, OCD, ODD, and all sorts of emotional and behavioral disorders, it all comes down to that extra chance or allowable mistake. Every kid needs to feel official and worth something, whether they know better or not (or are capable or not).

2. Be patient and kind, and kind and patient, and patient and kind.

In life, as in teaching, someone is always about to go off or melt down (students as well as teachers, as well as administrators), and the rewards are rarely immediate, but often long-lasting.

3. You might not be cut out for this.

If a teacher makes it past the *first* year, and then the *fifth* year, he or she may really be a teacher! I thought about quitting after my first year, and at that point I had been focused on nothing *but* being a teacher since I was seventeen. The job molds you and then owns you, and then, when you have tenure, *you* own the job.

4. Simplify, damn it.

Thoreau was mostly correct. All the important things in life have to do with getting the most out of situations where you're really focusing on the person, product, job, or question at hand. All I need for a class is a book, students who want to learn, and time. Nothing else, not even a Smartboard or Common Core Objectives.

5. "It all comes out in the wash"

…is what I've been saying for probably ten years, when I figured out that if a child is fed, can read, and has a trade (I have been fortunate to teach at a Tech school), then we've done our job. The rest is up to the storyteller and the protagonist.

6. Be excellent all the time, no matter what.

If you can't be excellent all the time, just learn how to edit your highlight reel, because as parents, children, writers, teachers, and workers, we maybe can't *always* be excellent. But that should be our standard, no matter what. My first mentor teacher always said "excellent" as her go-to adjective to her students and me, and every time she said this, I wanted to be excellent. I still do.

7. Just don't lose your shit.

You may lose your shit at some point, or a few points. I once lost it and yelled, "You're all chicken shithouse crazy!" Then we laughed about that for the rest of the year. What I said made no sense *and* made all sense in the moment. The students knew they were being crazy, and I had just had it. Life went on. But try not to lose it, especially near the chicken shithouse, whatever that means.

8. You only *die* once.

That's right. Forget *YOLO*, I'm talking about *YODO*. You live every day, but you will only die once (or twice if you are that rare case of being declared legally dead and then you get revived. Or a zombie). So here's my *Dead Poets' Society* moment of telling you to *Carpe Diem*, or, as I like to say, Carpe *Todayem*. Revise an essay to perfection; enjoy a book for once; be proud of mastering a project; relish that C+ you worked hard for. Now what you do with YODO is up to you, but be nice about it. Also, each class is experiencing you as a teacher for the *first time* each year, so you have time to change. And change. And change.

9. You *have* to commit.

There was a point in my third and fourth year of teaching that I had to have an out-loud talk with myself about being a teacher who does a bunch of *other stuff* on the side, or really being a teacher and committing myself to being the best teacher I could be without constantly focusing on better things. I chose to be an excellent teacher, or at least as excellent as I could be. And each year I have to commit myself again and again because you can't fake it until you make it. You just can't.

10. My kid is your kid for the year, and I'm teaching someone's kid.

Now that *my* children have teachers and *I'm* the one handing them over for seven plus hours a day, I feel the clarity of the situation: my students' parents are entrusting the greatest things in their lives to me for 200 plus hours a year. There are a few Golden Rules in that one, and I am so grateful that my kids have had excellent teachers so far. I don't ever want parents to dread the day their kid will have me in class.

11. Everybody needs an ambulance at some point.

I've put in plenty of "M's" (M is for Medical, and gives students time to finish work) on report cards for students who have had a bad case of Life making other plans for them. Some "M's" become "W's" (for Withdrawal, when Life hits the fan and breaks the ceiling) but some humans just need a few extra chances. Sometimes we need the gurney and the EMTs and the ambulance, and sometimes we just need a few extra weeks.

12. Hopefully we're getting better.

Each teacher meets the student where the student is able to be met, and nowhere else. Sometimes all the standards are thrown right out of the classroom. Sometimes that classroom is life, and sometimes that classroom is just a classroom. The nice thing about teaching is that every four years you get a clean slate with high schoolers, and you can feel free to grow and improve in different ways. The cycle of teaching life is always going, and every essay can be revised for a higher grade (that is, until the term is done).

13. Ask for help.

One of my go-to plays is saying *I Don't Know* to difficult student questions, then telling the students what I *do* know, and then talking about *and around* a problem. Sometimes I cite Antigone or Odysseus or Billy Pilgrim, and sometimes I just tell stories. But I've learned how to ask for help and whom to ask for help, and when to ask for help. And I will continue asking for help in different ways until the state-mandated robots make me clean out my room and retire early.

I've been *chicken shithouse crazy* plenty of times, but I'm still doing the wash.

And there's the bell. Here's to another twenty years and then some. I've been the luckiest in that I've had great teachers, and known great teachers, and hopefully, to the first twenty years of students, *been* a great teacher, at least on one of those many days I've paced the room with chalk in hand.

Han Solo, Captain Picard, or Mr. Spock? How to Decide What to Do in Life (When You Don't Know What To Do)

WE ALL FACE A HUNDRED DECISIONS a day from what to feed the kids to whether or not we should have that third beer.

The question of the essential self and how we want to portray ourselves can be simplified—sometimes.

But when that isn't enough, try this short list of what to do in those times of peril when you're wondering who can help guide us through each shadowy valley.

These archetypes are the stars of our own updated Anglo-Saxon Heroic poems, but with modern sensibilities that consider selflessness as a guiding virtue, whether or not the characters are aware of it at the time.

We should all be so fortunate.

What would Han Solo do?

Act like Han Solo. Or Indiana Jones.

Rough, rugged, skeptical, pirate-like Han was always my go-to growing up, rather than the bratty, whiny, privileged-with-Jedi-powers-he-somehow-overlooked-until-he-was-much-older towhead gringo Luke Skywalker (some farm boys have it all, and by "have it all" I mean endowed by birth with the power to rule the galaxy, or not).

Han shoots another scoundrel before getting hit himself, outruns a mafia boss, helps the good guys (acting as the deus ex machina) fight the Man (the Helmeted Man, that is), stays loyal to his co-pilot and best friend (without ever betraying him, as pirates do), suffers the torture of being frozen alive, and gets the girl respectfully after she saves him (she being the only girl in an entire universe, it seems, except for some of Jabba's dancers).

At first Han appears to be woefully trapped inside the typical "Man-Box" of machismo stereotypes, but over and over he lays down his life for his friends as if it was his job. He grows as a character, like the worst and best of us.

Then "he" (considering the viewer, always) hops franchises and becomes another iconic character, Indiana Jones, a somewhat morally pure professor whose line "this belongs in a museum" is simply crawling with good intentions for stolen, privatized goods that an aboriginal culture may or may not have been worshipping at the time.

He is wise and naive, loving yet distant, loyal, and again, grows as he learns, all the while crafting a great guiding directive for how to think about material things and wealth.

Plus he outsmarts millennia of gold-seekers as to what cup Christ would have sipped from, just to save his dad.

Be either of those guys. Chewie isn't so bad either.

What would Spock do?

Act like Spock. When in doubt of what to do or who to be in life, act like Spock. Sorry, Kirk.

In the Aristotelian rhetorical triangle of life, we all need to appeal to Logic a bit more, without committing the fallacy of only appealing to logic a little more. In that logic, good luck finding the logic in only ascribing to Logic. That's why we have the Kirks of the world, but I never liked Kirk, so I'm going with a modified Spock. And Spock was modified because he was half-human and half-Vulcan. He was the go-to adviser, and always knew the right answer.

Spock is a nonviolent (except in self-defense) vegetarian who will outlive all of his friends, and part of a race of Vulcans who were once barbarians. Aside from the awful haircuts and ears, sign me up.

Do you always know the right answer? If not, just channel Spock through a hands-free mind-meld, and you'll be alright.

What would Picard do?
Make it so. Just make it so.

When was the last time you took on an Ultra-God and a race of cyborg killers? And it was on your very first mission, nonetheless? You think life is hard? What, you've got needy kids and you're tired? Your job is hard and your days are long? Try being Picard. Seriously, try it. Or assume what it's like, call upon his center-bald spirit, make that hot Earl Grey, and decide. Make it so.

Maybe you're constantly being called on the carpet for crimes against humanity or dealing with the demons of having been possessed by a technological communist-zombie cult (draw appropriate metaphors wherever), but, in the end, if you rely upon your indomitable, stubborn spirit for adventure and truth (and the right thing, above all else), your Number One, and a solid crew of tried-and-true professionals, you'll make it out okay in the end.

Hell, Beverly Crusher will wait years for you to book that Holodeck vacation so you two can finally get together.

Finally—every day—what would you do?
Eventually in life you're going to have to forego your heroes (real or fictional) and what they will, would, or won't do, and just do you. There is no try—there is only do. And when you do, don't doodoo.

Doodoo is a big metaphor here, not just a quick joke. Seriously—don't doodoo. The world is full of it and we don't need any more.

And remember that all these characters were real people and had stable, steady lives where they were married and spent a good time raising multiple children in the real world.

Who Are You When No One Else Is Looking?

OUR BRAINS ARE SELF-SERVING, deceptive, and wonderful things. They reflect and produce, create and interpret, and analyze each concrete and abstract point and symbol from life so as to comfort itself, prolong life, and survive. We think we're *good*—we really do—even when we're not objectively good, and we rewrite history as much as we can, often employing others to echo our version of events, whether it's a bowling score, some "glory days" narrative, or a nation's treatment of its disenfranchised people. We're just like that, us humans.

And who we are—whoever that is—is who we are when we are alone and don't think we're being watched, when our thoughts echo and secret plans are made for the day, or month, or lifetime.

Observing the Observer

My children's brains—much like yours and mine—already run on intermittent loops of how to act and think *in light* of dad (and mom), figuring in what I did wrong (and the times I forgot about it). Somehow their little brains' dendrites locked onto a million small moments I wasn't aware of or didn't think of; they'll remember what dad was doing when they were busy playing and I thought they weren't listening, or what it was like to ask me questions, hold my hand. They've been cataloging my brand of discipline and attitude and cross-referencing it with every other parent, adult, teacher, and child, since ever. Almost all of this can be said for my decade-plus years of students and athletes, who were always observing the observer.

The question here is: *Who are you when no one else is looking?* Aside from asking my parents, wife, students, former roommates, and people in close proximity who I didn't know *were* looking, I'm all alone in answering this, fittingly. And so are you.

Only Children are Strange Creatures

As an only child, I had years of practice being myself when no one was looking, and, thanks to great musical and theatre training, plenty of years of also performing on stage and in the classroom, when others *were* looking. Thankfully I didn't develop the unique narcissism that plagues many only children. I *did* develop a sense that I'm *supposed* to be great, for some reason, and that odd guilt, in part, drives me, along with a propensity to perform. It's a part of me that's stuck as far as who I am, although I fight hard against such unnatural pressures (just ask my two therapists).

"There is nothing you must be, and there is nothing you must do," goes my favorite Zen saying, which is one of the hardest ideas to grasp and internalize in a world of heavy must dos and who-be's. Everyone is someone, right? But everyone can't be greater than everyone else. So you must be great at being you. Or something like that.

The hardest part of acting on stage is when you're *not* delivering lines. You're just there, in character, acting like a character, standing like a character, breathing like a character, waiting for lines. The You that is *really* You is the You who is inside your actions; you are also the sum of your reactions; you are as complex and simple as the next observer and the thoughts you think when you're reflecting on your performance, either as a character or as *your* character, whoever that is.

You are complex, and multitudinous, and yet you and I are only a little loose dirt

When no one is looking I'm often practicing for when they are, but also trying to enjoy being alone, which I do enjoy. As a writer I'm hoping for an audience who wants to read what I'm thinking about when no one else is looking; as a teacher and coach I want to be observed when no other teacher or administrative person is observing, because that's when I'm most natural and hopefully most effective and true; as a parent I want to be *present* at all times, and kind and smart with my kids, even if they aren't paying any attention (sometimes I can actually leave the room and they don't notice!); and as a husband I want to be the same loving friend at all times, whether we're catching a quick conversation while the kids are distracted, or whether we're hiding from the kids to be alone *together*, or, on that rare occasion when we get to go out, I want to be the ideal and imperfect person my wife wanted to – and did – marry.

But when no one is actually looking, I don't want to just be preparing to *not* be alone. I want to be, and I am, hooked into the same channels I've been locked into since my memory-making machine first kicked in years ago. "I'm the same as I was when I was six years old," goes the lyric from Modest Mouse, and I agree. I feel the same "me" as I remember feeling at age three and thirteen and thirty-three. There is something, some layered creature that I feel that is decidedly *me*, all the time, anywhere, with or without another. My wit + intelligence + memories + proclivities + kindness + anger + curiosity + earnestness + ability to function in a group + a bunch of x, y, and z factors = a good *base* for who I am, and then how I react *when no one is looking* gives me insight into what I truly am, beyond just being a good and kind person. I actually aim to be the same whether someone is looking or not, and I'm well aware of who might be looking.

But who you are transcends easy Venn diagrams and a whole existence based on one choice.

Life is full of *nobody* looking at you
This is true most of the time, most places, even on Google Earth. Everyone needs to be alone as much as possible in order

to recharge and center. Sometimes that centering comes when there's a crowd, and sometimes it happens in the quieter moments of meditation while watching reruns or doing nothing (there's much to be said for doing nothing, as it were). A third of your life is sleeping and dreaming, when only your own subconscious and unconscious abilities are watching what your *other* subconscious and unconscious talents are doing or undoing. The other two-thirds of your life are spent with minimal watching, because most people are observing themselves, or the 2D characters on TV or in books.

Maybe no one is watching you because there are just too many people to watch. That might be a good thing.

Who you are, in public and private, is a grandiose thing, whatever it is.

And sometimes it happens–a perfect development of who you actually are–only when the children are watching or listening, making those films in their perfect little brains.

So who are *you* when no one else is looking?

Start Every Day of Your Amazing Life with the Following...

YOU ARE A MAGICAL, wondrous collection of years of selection.

If you are alive, you've beat out millions of possibilities for a chance at your life in a universe slightly tilted in your direction as a living, sentient, self-aware individual.

If you've survived gestation, infancy, babyhood, childhood, adolescence, and part of adulthood, and especially any part of older age (or any combination of these), then you're literally at the top of the human game—you've made it.

If you have someone you love, children, a best friend, or family—even for a short time—then you know what it means to be alive and to discover the things that give life meaning.

If you can read, have a home, are well fed and mostly healthy, and want for almost nothing serious in life, you're doing better than many people on Earth now and most of those who have lived since day one of humankind.

And you have lived longer than possibly 90 percent of all humans since the beginning of time and space.

Even the animals don't live as long as you.

So get busy living, in the moment, all day long.

Just in from the Future: The Coming War Should Have Never Happened

AT WHAT POINT WILL WE have to fight with sticks and rocks because there is nothing left to destroy and no working machinery to use?

Alas, this simple message just came in either from the near, far, or distant future—which one we don't know.

It could also be from any time in the past—wartime or not.

Country of origin, whether colony or empire, we also don't know.

But we, as men, never heed its message.

Why? We'll never know.

And we'll never learn enough to know.

Or will we?

Read, listen.

Listen:

The _____ war you're currently hoping for— as all men hope for war in some strange optimism that only humans consciously possess—or at least hoping to enter at some point as heroes (whether secretly or openly) will be very and detrimentally bad for everyone involved, especially children, the elderly, certain ethnic and religious groups, and the Earth itself. We're talking criminally, categorically, scorched-Earth-burnt-dirt-bad-shit awful.

The _____ war will easily benefit the top 15 percent of all economic groups worldwide at the sacrifice of most of the bottom 15 percent. The middle 70 percent will also suffer from the hellish business of nations hurting other nations in varying degrees. It's all we've ever known.

Everyone will have to deal with the fallout from the _____ war, and whoever is saying that war is good is willingly forgetting all the people who will die or lose loved ones and that kind of thing.

There are many alternatives to war, and people are employing them most of the time in their communities, schools, worship centers, and businesses, but for some reason you all love a good fight to the death, and celebrate the murdering that always brings said deaths. All those quotes about war being hell and all that? They're all true.

So please avoid the _____ war at all costs and reconsider any more bloodshed.

Sincerely,

The Future

To My Children, Who are Not Transgender

My Loves,

No amount of superstition, legislation, or public opinion could separate me from loving you and protecting you and providing you with a life that makes you happy, free, kind, and non-violent.

Every day of your life since you were old enough to go to school I have told you to be good and do good—to be kind, helpful, generous, gentle, awesome, and excellent.

You know that I love you no matter what and this applies to every situation there is.

So whatever you feel that you are, whatever you choose to be, and whatever you appear as to those who look on with judgment, I will be there to help you walk tall, be proud, and live your truth.

There are plenty of people out there in the world who—given the chance—would gladly stop you or protest the means of you becoming who you really are and reaching your full potential.

Are they bad people? No. They're just misguided and don't mind saying hurtful things. In fact, some of them are really nice people when you get to know them. Some of them live in our town, and some of them are in our family.

And if they got to know you—really know you for the amazing kids you are—they might not be so loud and hurtful about other kids just like you who are just trying to be the best kids they can be.

Because we know better.

And there are plenty of kids just like you who need friends who know how to be loving, compassionate, and understanding. The world is full of people—you never know who you're going to meet and befriend.

You're going to meet different types of classmates and neighbors who might dress or act differently, and you must always try to be a friend and get to know who they really are inside their brains and hearts.

So it's up to you, kids.

Not a world full of protestors can change my mind on this. And trust me, they try and try.

But we know better.

Love,

Dad

I'm Sorry, Thoreau: Men, Nature, and the Awful, Rotten World We've Created

I'M SORRY, HENRY. I TRIED.

We all tried. Well, some of us. Make that a whole hell of a lot of us *didn't* try—the Industrial Revolution and the Single-Use/Plastic-Styrofoam Throwaway Revolution have devastated the oceans and rolling plains beyond remedy and there's nothing I can do. We traded in simple living so the railroads, factories, and satellites could ride us. As a world, we gave up family farming for having cell phones so we could watch television on the toilet. Seriously.

I reduce as much as I can. I really do. Ask any of my family members, friends, or students, they'll all tell you the same: I'm some sort of a part-time fool for Nature conservancy.

But I can't do it anymore. I'm a city boy. I'm writing on a computer made of plastic and wires and conflict minerals (with nine tabs and five applications open), and I realize you have no idea what I'm talking about, since you're still existing in a pre-Civil War era America -- but essentially at some point in the last century, the whole world became addicted to convenience and easy use, and we couldn't get enough of all the polymers and minerals we took from the Earth (the upside is that our Health Industry today could have saved you from Tuberculosis with a plastic syringe and the right vaccine). We use those metals and materials to make accelerated computing devices, food trays, and, well, everything, but only using them for a few seasons because we build things to eventually break so that we can sell you a slightly better version. It's all planned.

Then we throw them away, where they end up in what's called a landfill, which is a big field of garbage covered with grass.

And cars too (large, mechanical carriages that go up to 120 miles-per-hour and run on gas and oil, which are mined from the Earth) —and buildings, and cows, and, well—there's nothing I can do, Henry. We've invented ourselves into oblivion—all too confidently, and although creating these things aligns nicely with your assertion to build foundations under our dreams, we've dreamt ourselves into a world full of waste.

The woods are burning, or far from pristine. And we're not going there deliberately anymore because we have theme parks and inside-superstores. But if I took you to Costco, you'd either flip your lid or fall in love. I know, I had the same reaction.

Convenience won. We are the ants and pygmies and cranes, fighting the creations we have made which will, if we breathe, drink, and live among the waste they create, destroy us.

But you knew that.

I've done a shitty job at simplifying. We all have—unless you consider a huge agriculture-corporation trademarking the seeds, food, and pesticides, and that same company putting the real farmers out of a job. That is simplicity!

My life—most peoples' lives now—is more complicated than any one of the patchwork Transcendentalist or Universalist philosophies. My DVR alone would shame me in a conversation with you, Henry. Seriously, if I were to explain all the time I spend watching televised theater, and how important it is to my life and the lives of my wife and children, I wouldn't be worth the paper stock they wrote my Master of Arts in English on.

And the Earth. The poor, wretched Earth.

In the years since you lived at Walden Pond (where I bring my students every year to ditch their computing devices and meditate and just get lost in the woods if they can ignore the railroad, highway, constricts of time, and other people), we've taken everything useful out of the Earth and used it up once and thrown it away again. We've polluted every sea and oceanic gyre between the seas, and we've raised the temperature of Earth just by emitting smog on the way to work.

Maybe it's better you're not here to scold me. But if you were, we could leave it all behind for the day, bake some bread, skinny dip in Walden Pond, and watch some ants fight on a hill. You could teach me how to identify plants and grow beans. And then we could debate on the front porch before I introduce you to television.

I have some amazing Nature documentaries to show you.

How a Pacifist Teacher Prepares His Students for War

"GO AND TEACH JEREMY HOW TO play with G.I. Joes," I remember a relative saying to one of my older cousins when I was six.

I had just received my first G.I. Joe action figure and I was already well-versed in the world of Star Wars toys, although the small guns that came with them weren't allowed in my pacifist home. My cousin introduced me to the soldier leader toy, "Duke," and I was hooked—like any child would be.

There is something life-altering for a young boy when he holds his first toy soldier and learns to maneuver, shoot, and maim (although all fans of similar toys and their TV show related franchises know that somehow cartoons never actually suffer).

Toy soldiers never die, you know.

I knew my father would object because we had a strict "no guns" policy when it came to toys; a decade earlier he had stood up against the Vietnam War as a conscientious objector after being first in the draft, and was handed his papers to be shipped off to war. He refused service before a judge, married, and lived, working for the state to stave off his service. I was born a few years later.

In my adulthood I also chose nonviolence as a philosophy, borrowing from Tolstoy, Thoreau, Gandhi, Dr. King, and a host of heroes and heroines who simply said and say no to all violence. As a high school teacher, however, I am often challenged with the reality that my students—who I admire, cherish, and would save from death if I could—join the Armed Forces and are called to violence across the world.

For my generation, there has been no great war—men and women my age escaped a large statist calamity, only to have the slightly *next* generation suffer at the hands of lawyers-turned-statesmen who ushered us into more than a decade of "real" war in the Middle East.

But high school kids—especially those who live in the city where I teach—are often prime real estate for an all-volunteer army that always needs soldiers. Why do we always send the poor? Because it's what we've always done.

1, 2, 3, 4, we don't want your endless war...

It's one of those things that will always exist as a rite of passage: young, unmolded children seek reformation and maturation, meet military recruiter, and somewhere between junior year and graduation we have taller, leaner, more polite students with a fire in their eyes. Something is built, and goes, and is replaced, and the student is forever changed.

I have a special affinity for my soldier students—by graduation they're filled with ambition and obedience, although I know it's a specific cultish kind, like prep school or religion, a means to an end, where they will call me sir when they don't need to because they were taught to call me sir. Other students will mature slowly through existential trials and college and early parenthood, without the uniform or world-traveling. There's an excitement to this, that you can learn a trade, be someone, *and* serve your country, all at the expense of an occupation or—as the Gods always demand—endless war. I'd rather have my students growing out their stubble and falling out of love in college or some post-high school dreary job than this reality, but because I love my students and I value their freedom to choose their own path in life, I would never stand in their way. And yes, I understand that most soldiers never see action, and that for many of them it is a peaceful career that they and their families are proud of.

I'm usually proud as well, and eager to hear about their journey.

In part, this has trained me as a father, in that I won't always like what my children choose, and I won't always be able to sit well with it. But I will still have to be supportive and pleasant, even though the risks can outweigh the rewards, and leave us all with a flag-draped coffin and a quiet afternoon of reflection. Most careers are buffered by nonviolence on almost all sides, even if they're built on violent starts or betting. Soldiering is never one of them.

Soldier worship

In America, we worship the soldier, sports star, and celebrity with such reckless abandon it's hard *not* to want to be one or the others. But the soldier is always the *real* celebrated hero and heroine, with service, grit, and humility as credentials, as the hero-worship narrative goes. My young soldiers are asked to take life, protect it, and trade it all within moments of a leader's decision, all at the detriment of any lesson we covered in *Slaughterhouse-Five, Brave New World, 1984, Lord of the Flies*, or *Things Fall Apart*. All that retribution we should avoid between the Montagues and Capulets? It's okay if your country asks it of you. Odysseus' travels in Hades, encountering his enemies, friends, and family members, who could have avoided death if not for war? Forget the lesson, you've got your marching orders.

I abhor violence in every form—against men, women, and children, in prisons and the streets, in schools and against the animals and the Earth. Gang, mafia, and group violence is intolerable, however socially justified, and even more-so reprehensible when it is statist-sponsored, often against its own, but most popularly celebrated *by* its own against strangers across fields and towns and seas. And as far as justice is concerned, I do not wish my enemies—or those needing punishment—*any* corner of any hell. (I don't have any enemies, for one, and I don't believe in any hell.) If beatings and murder have taught us anything, it's that the beatings and murder don't work.

But the hero worship continues, and I get it. I understand that the desire to *be something* is so tangible in the armed services, especially when you're 16. The threat of death is real, but what teenager doesn't feel invincible? And the reality is that most soldiers will never have to use a weapon, although what teenager wouldn't want to?

I still don't want them to go. I don't want them to spend bullets on the armies and children of our enemies, because they were just children a few days ago, shuffling into my classroom and complaining about every appropriate thing teenagers should complain about.

I just want them to stay alive. And I want the people in foreign lands—those students of other teachers and sons and daughters of other parents—alive too, for as long as possible.

Standing before the gates of Hell

As a middle schooler, I received the heaviest education about the Holocaust by visiting the concentration camp site at Auschwitz-Birkenau and touring Europe while performing *I Never Saw Another Butterfly* with the American Boychoir School. As a young man, I learned invaluable lessons about life from Holocaust survivors and was privileged enough, at the same time, to live in a nonviolent house, neighborhood, and part of the city, although my hometown is known for violence against its own.

War, I learned at a young age, is something we *used* to do, and now we've learned our lesson. Only history has taught us that, if we've learned anything from history, it's that we've learned nothing from history. But as I became a man I saw the world justify new wars and skirmishes as if they had never existed, and as if no one had ever figured out how diplomacy works.

The insanity of war and genocide numbed me to any kind of narrative of soldier-saving-anyone, as it did to the narrative of the heroics of war in general. War is never kind, and anyone who has lived through one would never recommend it to anyone. Just ask the dead, or their survivors.

Children around the world need education, not militaries

At one point we had over forty violent gangs and crews in the city where I love to teach, and throughout the years, I've taught and counseled current and former gang members who want nothing to do with violence, but have to accept that it is simply part of the game and life. There is almost no long-term protection once a group has decided that violence is an option that it is allowable, and dependable; no one should have to live in the shadow of this fear, but yet it is the reality for children city, state, and worldwide. And when that group has unlimited nuclear weapons at its disposal, the unlimited worship of its citizens, and leaders who are willing to trade the lives of my students for any kind of assumed threat, I'm going to always have to say no.

This gum-chewing English teacher just loves his students too much to trade them for some skirmish in some foreign country. There are too many lives to save right here in the homeland.

I wish for the children of the world to be as educated as my students and children are and will be, from pre-K to twelfth grade, taught not to raise guns and blindly follow uniformed leaders, but to have the freedom to choose a way out of poverty other than a militarized reality. I'd rather see 16-year old soldiers around the world be bored in the classroom and worried about pimples and track meets than brainwashed by religion and militarism. But sadly, education is not the first thing dictators and leaders with guns look to in order to raise up a powerful people.

No one—student or otherwise—needs to die for me
"It's been my dream to be a Marine since I was young," one student claimed in a heartfelt class conversation before a recent senior graduation. This student, a pupil of mine since he was fresh out of middle school, has grown into a self-aware man, full of potential, wit, and wisdom. And now, like many of my students, he has been broken down, built back up, and is a Marine. I want him to live a long life, full of beauty, success, and learning. He will now always be a Marine, but more importantly, he will also always be my student, even though he's graduated.

During the same conversation, we—a class including several students going off to basic training for the Army, Navy, and Marines, as well as plenty of students who never considered any of it—talked about the need for fighting, violence, revenge, and justice. Very coolly we arrived at the fact that people will always want to fight, and there will always be people who want to defend and make it their business to serve, whether it calls for violence or not. In that moment I remember being at peace with my students who were going off to become soldiers, as if I had finally let go of the fact that, at the heart of life and civilization, there will always be students going off to war, and there will always be teachers wishing for more time with them in the classroom, where we can be safe from battle and harm's way.

"When you're out there about to assassinate someone, shoot high, and let him live," I told another one of my students, half-jokingly, before he went off to basic training, which included specialized sniper education, for which he later performed. He ended up never firing at any targets during his time in the service while always awaiting the order to do so.

He's still alive, for now, in a second career, as are most of my former soldier students, and I hope they will be for a long life full of joy, prosperity, and happiness.

You Don't Have To Worry So Much (and Some of the Answers for Now)

THE "SOME OF THE ANSWERS FOR NOW" or "You Don't Have To Worry So Much" advice pile/small book of proverbs that follow started as seven pieces of advice I wrote down the night before my first day teaching and then added to that May as my first batch of seniors walked toward freedom. I was twenty-two, many of them nineteen. I think I amassed a total of thirty pieces of advice by the next year, and soon that thirty became fifty, fifty became a hundred, and then my lid totally flew off and I just kept reducing the font and filling up two columns of words that could fit on one page, double sided (all that were literally fit to print). This list is the last thing I do with my seniors, which now takes about sixteen minutes to read, and includes almost all of the advice I can think of.

However, a disclaimer, a warning: reading this list won't save you. Your life won't be complete upon finishing the last item. It won't even touch the depth of turmoil that will twist your brain and break your ass throughout your adult life. But it might help. And it might feel good to read.

Enjoy.

* * *

You Don't Have to Worry So Much (Some of the Answers for Now, for All Graduates This and Every Spring)

1. Keep Right.
2. You can have everything you need and want in life. Just ask.
3. Imitation is important, but we all need an original hero. That's you.

4. Don't worry so much about the future—it will be there when you arrive.

5. The only thing you have in life is this present moment, so don't waste it.

6. Some of you should relax. You know who you are; some of you should stop relaxing. You know who you are.

7. Follow your heart; follow your mind as well. Sometimes you won't know what to do—in this case, follow your feet.

8. Follow your dreams, and then push your dreams to follow you. Get started now.

9. Ahh_l spellinngh; gramerend puncutation, And capatalisadion mus bee NR purfek..CORECT N CLAIR COMUNIKATION MATRRSS

10. Tell your family and friends you love them—often.

11. Respect and be good to your parents—one day you will be them, or better. And call your mother.

12. Everything to everyone is always happening. So get busy living.

13. When it rains, you may get wet—be prepared; when things burn, you may get burnt—be prepared; if you're not prepared, be prepared to not always be prepared.

14. Everyone thinks they're better, wiser, or smarter than the next one. Fight against this.

15. Get smart as much and as often as possible. Always keep smartening up.

16. Wisdom and youth aren't always worn on the right bodies--so be young and wise when you can.

17. Write something brilliant for us to read, and read something brilliant as much as possible.

18. The grass is sometimes greener somewhere else, but there is only so much green one can handle. Avoid lawn envy.

19. Try vegetarianism at least once. The animals and planet will never thank you, but you'll be healthier for it.
20. Take care of the Earth, plants, animals, and children -- we need them as much as they need us.
21. Love each other. If you can't love each other, at least try to like each other. If you can't like each other, then get to know each other, and take it from there.
22. The fact that you think you know what you think you know doesn't always mean you really know. You know?
23. You never know—unless you do, but even then: you never know.
24. Watch out for people who know everything—You may be one of them.
25. Don't settle for either happiness *or* labor--sometimes the trade makes you and sometimes you just have it made.
26. Sometimes you will need an ambulance, and sometimes you will just need a tall glass of water.
27. Sometimes you will make a fool out of yourself. It's okay.
28. Sometimes doing nothing works best. Sometimes it doesn't.
29. Sometimes money fixes a problem, sometimes it doesn't.
30. Learn to respect what you don't understand, and then try to understand.
31. Listen carefully when listening; talk carefully when talking; feel carefully what you feel.
32. You are extremely important, official, and powerful in every way imaginable. Respect that.
33. You *belong*—as weird, cool, wonderful, awful, different, smart as you are—here, now, forever.

34. You are the only one who can make a difference in your own way, and nobody will ever take your place. Know that.
35. Whatever you're going through, keep going.
36. Remember that people are just people and that everybody has to eat and we're all just trying to get home; we're all in this together most days (some of us reluctantly)
37. Falling in love often involves tripping and, actual falling, so be careful who you take with you.
38. Respect and demand respect in all areas of love and desire.
39. There are several "someones" out there, waiting to love you completely—and some who won't. Happy hunting!
40. Everything and everybody is connected, whether they're connected or not.
41. All persons, living and dead, are purely coincidental.
42. Be careful of who you give control of your life to—and be careful of who takes it, whether they ask or not.
43. Be aware of the pain and suffering in the world, and work hard to ease as much of it as you can.
44. Be here now (wherever "here" is) and explore the present moment. That's really all there is.
45. Be careful of who you give the best of yourself to. Not everyone deserves your best.
46. Be as fair as you can to those around you, even when it doesn't benefit you—
47. Fight for the freedom of everyone, even when it doesn't benefit you.
48. Be as kind and as generous as you can without expending yourself.
49. Be careful what you wish for, you might just get it.
50. Be as free as you can be without causing any harm.

51. Be the answer you hope to find in this world.
52. Be a friend—everybody needs one.
53. Be yourself, whoever that is.
54. Be nice. Just. Be. Nice.
55. Try to waste nothing.
56. Simplify.
57. Know when to lay low and know when to make waves, and know when to say no to both, or when to float.
58. Everybody needs somebody. Know when to be that somebody.
59. Do as much good as you can for as many people as you can right this instant.
60. Choose which judgment days to live in light of.
61. Each day, pick one thing not to worry about.
62. ...And yes, you don't have to worry so much.
63. Try to do one thing at a time. Just try it.
64. Know when to work hard; know when to work smart; know when to rest.
65. There is no laziness as good as the reward of hard work.
66. Feel free to fart around when you can. Naps are good, too.
67. *Things you'll be better for:* getting outdoors as much as you can, enjoying and demanding a good cry from yourself now and then, keeping a journal when and where you can, taking time each day to be alone with your thoughts.
68. Avoid violence, complaint, and insult, and you will live all your days in peace.
69. We are all one step away from where we don't want to be, so watch your step.
70. Clean up after yourself. You never know who will follow.
71. Never betray the ones you love, including yourself.

72. Let go of anger—it holds you more than you hold it.
73. Try to notice when someone gets a new haircut.
74. Always tip 20% or better.
75. Never jangle your car keys near sewer grates.
76. Laugh as much as you can without causing a scene.
77. You're going to forget and/or sleep through most of the one life you get, so be ready to be alive every day.
78. Get involved in your community every chance you can.
79. Remember where you came from—it may just be the right place.
80. Please remember that "please" and "thank you" go a long way. Thank you.
81. Vote every chance you can, either on election days or with your wallet any other day.
82. Learn how to dance; learn how to laugh at yourself (these two are not exclusive to each other).
83. Learn how to write well. Some of us want to know your ideas.
84. Learn how to sing well. If you can't sing, learn an instrument. Then sing along.
85. Learn how to saunter properly.
86. Take care of your body—you only get one, and maybe assorted parts someday.
87. Take care of yourself—we can't be a good *we* without *you*.
88. Know that you become less attractive the more you complain.
89. Know yourself, flaws and all.
90. Know when to be satisfied—there is nothing better than a satisfied mind. *Getting* there is the anxious part.
91. When you're older you'll tell kids to respect their elders, so get started now.

92. Failure can teach us more than success. Be willing to learn either way.

93. Once fear is allowed in, it becomes boss. Work hard against this...and if you can avoid fear and ego, you've won at life.

94. Avoid psychopaths, cheats, liars, and narcissists, and avoid being any of them as well.

95. Always be humble and kind. Always.

96. Hope does not always spring eternal. But it should.

97. Practice doesn't make perfect, it makes *permanent*.

98. Know that so much depends on self-reliance.

99. Meet the Transcendent where and when you can— even if it's only in a conversation.

100. Don't just look smart, be smart.

101. Don't be afraid to fight for the right thing. Don't be afraid to run, either.

102. Don't forget to breathe.

103. Don't just *believe* in yourself, but *accept* yourself, doubt and all.

104. Don't believe everything you read, hear, and see.

105. Don't believe everything you think, either.

106. Don't be afraid of the Big Questions; don't be afraid of the small answers, either.

107. Don't be afraid to suffer for the right reasons—life, in fact, is full of them. Life is also full of suffering.

108. Don't lionize the wrong lions—smaller creatures need their place too.

109. When you see the tiger, avoid the tiger—unless you're *ready* for the tiger, or you *are* the tiger.

110. Sometimes you eat the bear, and sometimes the bear eats you. O my.

111. Seek and beware of Truth and Beauty in the world around you.

112. Nothing divides us as much as our own point of view.
    -

113. Everyone is out for "number one," so decide who that "number one" truly is.
114. A broken clock is right twice a day, but it is still broken.
115. Words are more powerful than swords—they can cut years after spoken.
116. Never pass judgment on those who haven't had the privileges you've had.
117. If there is an extra mile to go, then go.
118. When Life gives you lemons, be glad it wasn't shit.
119. When Life gives you lemons, ask for water and sugar.
120. When Life gives you lemons, learn all you can about lemons.
121. Looking good < feeling good < being good < being good for something good.
122. Sometimes it's *not* all good—sometimes it is.
123. At some point you're going to have to be good at something and work hard. Don't be afraid to start now.
124. Avoid clocks and mirrors when you can.
125. Make friends with a library.
126. Read that book you've been wanting to read.
127. Figure out where your money goes. Then either chase it or help it get there.
128. Try hard not to love money, fame, power, or things.
129. What goes around sometimes really goes around.
130. It's okay to be wrong about things. Life is often lived between satisfaction and regret.
131. Forgive often and when you can. Try forgetting some things too.
132. If you always do the right thing, you'll always do the right thing.
133. Always be learning—education is life itself; always be reading for pleasure or enlightenment or both or

neither or other; always have a pen ready and a brain warmed.

134. Always be seeking adventure.

135. Always be improving; always be listening; always be honest, even when it hurts.

136. Always make new mistakes.

137. Always be mindful of those less fortunate and then do something about it. Take nothing for granted.

138. Always be deciding your fate. Sometimes you *can't* choose your way out of a situation. In that case, forge ahead with patience, humility, diligence, love, and compassion.

139. Always ask more questions; Always be going in peace;

140. Know when to let go; know when to hold on; know when to juggle. Practice healthy unattachment.

141. Numbers and titles and awards matter little, so seek the right things that will last.

142. Find your voice, but remember that people don't always listen.

143. Who you are today is always changing into who you are tomorrow—give yourself time.

144. Stay young—but not too young.

145. Whoever you become, wherever you are, whatever you do, in all things: *don't be an asshole*.

146. If this is all there is, let's make it the best "is" there is.

147. Consider the idea that there is nothing you must do or be, there is nothing you must have or know, and that there are no days in the weeks, or hours in the days, or years in your life. *Is* just is.

148. Love is the answer—so get busy finding the questions.

149. There is always a root to the root of the root. Start planting, and there is almost always another "why?" to ask. Keep asking.

150. Let that which truly matters, matter; let that which truly *doesn't* matter, *not* matter.
151. All the answers are right in front of you or somewhere around here. Keep searching.
152. You are the hero we've all been waiting for. So get to work.
153. Try your damnedest to live long and prosper without violence of any kind.
154. ...And when in doubt, see number one.

~In Love and Life, Mr. McKeen (May 2020)

Are You the Hero We're All Looking For?

F. SCOTT FITZGERALD WROTE of the pre-Gatsby James Gatz, "So he invented just the sort of Jay Gatsby that a seventeen year old boy would like to invent, and to this conception he was faithful to the end." It's this concept—that a seventeen year old would create a larger-than-life figure to grow into—that is the basis for every superhero tale from Gilgamesh to Harry Potter.

With a non-stop barrage of brilliant superhero series and movies coming at us, it is prudent to look at the archetypes that make every metahuman, mutant, demigod, and Time Lord worth their weight in adamantium. You are probably living an origin story right now, and soon you'll have more responsibility and power than you hoped for.

For starters: You're probably living in the city, an ambiguous 20-something, and single.

You're probably an orphan of some sort, and with a sad or mysterious story about being so. If you live in the country, you'll soon be somehow called into the city to meet some great fate, whether it be a dragon (or dragon archetype) or some interstellar artificial intelligence/alien. Either way, no superhero stays in the country (or country of origin). Almost every fight ends up on Earth, in America, and usually in New York City. So just move to New York City.

You're an introverted and somewhat—or totally—nerdy teen with a propensity for all things S.T.E.M.?

Is there a girl (or boy) who you just can't get? And are you a misfit or reject of some sort? Just wait – you'll be bit, zapped, or injected with gamma-rays or something radioactive, or your mutant powers will grow as your puberty finishes. Just wait for an owl to deliver a letter from a balding man, or a long-lost father to invite you to the dark side.

You happen to be a Goddess, God, Demigod, Planetary Traveler, Alien, Other-worldly royalty, or Interdimensional Being.

Do you have a legacy to uphold here on terra firma, while also fighting for your throne back home? You might just be on your way to join a superhero team or save Earth from the demons or villains who also happen to be from your home world. Or you might be orphaned on Earth. Or you might just hide out here because we have all the good movie and fast food franchises. Any way you slice it, you'll probably get the same billing as the normal human with the bow and arrow.

Can you run real damn fast? Like faster-than-a-jet fast? Like faster-than-DSL fast?

You're in. For some reason, every superhero tale or team needs a speedster. Sure, the alien superheroes can probably fly or run quickly, but somehow you're special because that's all you do. That's called focus. Now take our drink order   you can definitely beat the crowd to the bar.

Your silver spoon is showing: you're a super-rich tycoon who also happens to invent technology that even N.A.S.A. hasn't started dreaming up yet.

And you can build indestructible Magic and God-defying armored suits for everyone on the team. And if you have to, you'll take down the team, you know, when they get taken over by sorcery or alien mind-control. You probably already know that you're a superhero, and you didn't need me to tell you that.

For some reason, in today's post-industrial, cyber-focused world, you're an amazing archer.

You're also amazingly adept with any weaponry where you can shoot a bird in the eye from seventeen miles away, and you can afford stealthy outfits and staying up most nights a week guarding the city you love.

Scientists apply: most scientists end up as villains in the superhero world, but you may just transform into something greater in the lab, or near Earth's orbit.

If you think your doctorate and lab work doesn't count for much in terms of brute athleticism, think again: you could easily become a beast, thing, stretchy man, or whatever a "hulk" of mammalian mass is, without all that reason and logic to hold you back. But you *still* have the IQ of history's greatest thinkers. However, you'll need extra time under the Bodhi tree to keep that anger in check.

Are you a gritty individual who has lost loved ones to violence and you must now wander the Earth avenging their deaths (with or without weaponry you once swore off)? Or are you also maybe a top-level double-agent working for international shadowy agencies?

There's a special place for you in the superhero world, and chances are you will wear a lot of leather and wigs.

Job opening: former criminals, soldiers, and/or mercenaries who have seen the error of their ways and want to be magically or scientifically enhanced.

You might also be trying to save a loved one from a villain or government conspirators, or trying hard to make one last heist before you retire (when you realize you can use your talents for good). We take all kinds.

Finally, do you have any of the following: Magic or psychic powers, sovereignty over the elements, or invisibility? Were you once kidnapped by aliens or alien bounty hunters and given special weapons or abilities? Are you from the future? And do you have other powers yet addressed?

If so, you are at the beginning stages of what could be a solid series of adventures first on your own, then with a team or sidekick, then in parallel universes, then in obscurity, and eventually in many franchised books, television series, and films! You're on your way, old sport.

The Very Last and Definitive Word on "DadBod"

Wherein the writer is granted an interview with God and Mrs. God about the cultural idea that "dadbods" are "in" somehow.

JM: Thank you for having me. You have a lovely home.

GOD: It's no Mt. Olympus or the desert, but it gets really great Wi-Fi on a clear day and there's a new Starbucks drive-thru one town over.

Mrs. GOD: And he has his little shed where he can tinker.

GOD: And there's that. She has the garden too.

JM: So a lot of the blogosphere and the national media in the past few weeks have been obsessed with this new concept of "DadBod" which is essentially a man's somewhat flabby physique, vis a vis Leonardo DiCaprio and the average college age male with a little bit of a beer gut.

Mrs. GOD: Oh, yes, it's all the rage.

GOD: Kids these days. In my days, men were cut and women wore flowing robes and such.

Mrs. GOD: I blame it on jeggings. For centuries women were satisfied with layered linens and roped material, and now it's all yoga pants and bikinis.

JM: So you're aware of the "DadBod" obsession in the media?

GOD: We read the blogs. I was thinking of starting my own, but I don't want to have to pay for anything.

Mrs. GOD: I told him there are plenty of WordPress formats for free.

GOD: That's not what I was saying.

JM: So, seeing as you two are the progenitors of the human race, any input on body issues or the fact that "DadBod" is kind of a cute, kitschy thing while "MomBod" seems to be something to lose in time for the beach or a magazine cover? Or even hide?

Mrs. GOD: Well, let me take this one. I've given birth to roughly 400 billion souls, and if that doesn't give you a little tummy and some extra meat on the haunches, I don't know what will. Old Thunderbolt here has had his DadBod since forever.

GOD: It kind of goes with the beard. As long as you have broad shoulders and a little definition in the chest, women don't care.

Mrs. GOD: Don't get Him started.

GOD: I mean, what, I had my heyday. My appearance didn't matter. I once impregnated a woman while taking the form of a swan. And then there was that time with that girl from Nazareth. I'll never hear the end of that. (Awkward silence).

JM: And what about the double standard for women? Why do you think there is no "MomBod" fascination?

GOD: Look, if a man finds a female desirable, then what's the problem? Men are dirt bags. Literally, they're all made from dirt. But women, oh, there's something beautifully evil about them. They must be perfect. Women know that. Women even know that men don't really care what they look like, as long as they can show them off or give birth to warriors or other Demigods. Have you seen these trolls that pass for humans around Earth? These misshapen forms walking around texting all the time? The average man or woman–they're no cover models, I'll tell you. But men know that women know that men want the perfect shapes and all that, even as a fantasy, and that's how money is made. Women are either mothering men or trying to please them. As it should be.

Mrs. GOD: And -- well, I guess He's kind of right. So much smarter than His brothers.

JM: So it's just a marketing strategy? I mean, are you serious? What about equal rights and all that?

GOD: Everything is a marketing strategy. I had to evade being eaten by my own father. If my mother hadn't really sold that stone wrapped in a blanket to my dad, there'd be no Gods. Imagine a world without Gods! It'd be chaos.

JM: So as for DadBod, it's just a silly notion to make men feel better about being a little out of shape?

Mrs. GOD: Oh, of course. But that Seth Rogen, I like him. But it seems like he gets less funny in every movie that he makes. You know, he was thin for that *Green Arrow* movie.

GOD: It was the *Green Hornet*. And that Jason Segel is so talented, but always with the penis. In like every movie. I mean, I get it. But come on. Even I got tired of the Greeks always doing everything naked all the time.

JM: And what about the impossibly high standard for women post-baby? You can't pass a magazine stand without seeing a celebrity showing off her–and it's *always a her*–body a few months after having a baby.

GOD: I don't know. They sell ads. People need to buy whatever garbage they're selling these days. Again, men don't care. Women care. Women are a plague, but a well needed plague.

Mrs. GOD: Ugh. He's such a man. Let me tell you something, and I'm going to get deep here. Until maybe a hundred years ago, none of these humans were living very long, and since then and back through time and memoriam, most women were having babies at very young ages. Their bodies would bounce back. But today you all are living to be way too old and having babies later, when your metabolism has slowed to half-mast and then one-quarter-mast. If you have all your babies by the age of twenty, like we intended, there wouldn't be any DadBods or MomBods to be silly about. It's simple. Plus you all eat too much. Back in the day it was all wheat and lamb and olives. Now everything is full of sugar.

GOD: What? Look, my daughter, Helen, was the most beautiful woman on the planet. Started a ten year war. Who wouldn't want to look like her? She didn't run for president or cure scurvy; she was just pretty. The prettiest. All the men wanted her. She wasn't some Olivia Pope or Hillary Clinton character who has it all.

Mrs. GOD: These celebrities, it's all they have – their looks. Women are smart enough to know the difference. Well, some women. But celebrities aren't real people, so I'm not worried.

JM: So you follow the celebrity shows and culture?

Mrs. GOD: I watch from time to time, usually after the nightly news. I also watch the Kardashians and the Duggars every now and then when nothing is on.

GOD: Thankfully you can turn off Omniscience when you want. Ignorance is a blessing. (To Mrs. GOD) A whole world of opportunity and genius, though, and you watch this drivel?

Mrs. GOD: What? It's well produced.

GOD: I don't know how you keep track of them all.

Mrs. GOD: It's pretty easy, Dummy. Kim's the popular and most prettiest one with the sex tape and the big ass. And Kanye and the babies. The Duggars are the ones who can't stop having babies and getting married.

GOD: I know who they are. (GOD winks at the interviewer).

Mrs. GOD: And you could even say the Duggars beat the whole "MomBod" notion by wearing those awful denim form-covering clothes all the time.

GOD: Well, the whole world can't stop having babies and getting married. It's a whole thing, apparently.

JM: Ok, and while we're at it, any advice about marriage?

GOD: Well, we're not in a traditional marriage, so our whole thing works. But marriage is overrated. If you can find that special someone you don't want to cheat on or destroy, then it might just be true love. Or your sister. I'm really not the best one to ask about this.

Mrs. GOD: We're just a crazy old couple, keeping the Universe going.

JM: And specifically, on the topic of same-sex marriage in the U.S., I'm sure the public would love to hear your thoughts.

GOD: Well, marriage is between a man and his property, the way men intended it to be.

Mrs. GOD: You mean a woman and her property.

GOD: Exactly.

JM: And–I have to ask–could you put an end to all of the suffering in the world?

GOD: Oh, that old chestnut. Mortals have been asking that for eons. Well, you seem nice. I'm sure you'll figure it out. But most of these humans, they just fight about every little thing, no matter what the option or solution. It's like you're cursed to be the way you are.

Mrs. GOD: There's only so much we can do. We're not really hands-on entities unless there's a big war or something.

JM: So there's nothing you can do?

GOD: Well, we're not genies. You all were like an afterthought. We're surprised you kept things going like you did! You're all going to Hades anyway, so it doesn't matter. I mean, I say that in the nicest way possible. Everybody goes to Hades when they die. It's awful. So enjoy your time here now.

Mrs. GOD: Except for all the pollution and wars, you mortals have done a great job. Well, we Gods kind of enjoy the wars. It's like March Madness for us.

JM: Well, thank you for your time.

GOD and **Mrs. GOD:** Anytime.

My Wife, Six Lesbians, and I Walk Into a Hooters

STOP ME IF YOU'VE HEARD THIS ONE BEFORE: A vegetarian, his wife, and six lesbians walk into a Hooters.

No?

I've been to Hooters twice, and both times happened to be with a group of close friends (the lesbians) and my wife, all while I was still a vegetarian. I know, I know, these jokes write themselves. It was more a geographical anomaly rather than a conscious decision. Suffice to say it was awful and uncomfortable, like a married vegetarian going to Hooters with his wife and a table full of lesbians. That should sum it up nicely, yes? If my mother and grandmothers had been there, I would have a better joke for you.

It's not that I couldn't have fun or relax that night—who am I kidding? I couldn't have fun or relax. I couldn't escape my heterocentricity. Or my vegetarianism (has the world really not figured out solid vegetarian options for every restaurant by this point?). It was just awkward, as progressive and liberal and judgement-free as we are, there are some things that just—for good reason—make you awkward.

The lesbians—they loved it. They were there for the same reason as anyone who is attracted to women in flesh-colored stockings and form-flattering t-shirts would be. My wife, not so much. Yes, women walk around all the time in form-fitting clothes, or—at the beach I hate so much—in essentially padded underwear. Yes, we see them. But we're not always paying them to lean over to pour beer into frosty mugs. Sometimes we pay bartenders to do that.

No, I don't have a Princess Leia fetish

Most movies that men and women my age grew up with (and into) featured endless heterosexuals and one token female—a courtesy not even granted now to the Minions (even the Smurfs had a single Smurfette). For example, until recently we had a whole Star Wars universe of men with only a handful of females, one of whom had a Jedi for a father *and* brother, yet had no powers herself and ends up in a sexy slave outfit (until recently, where an older version can also use the Force). The same went for Star Trek, Indiana Jones, and every movie that still makes adults my age set the DVR. Every female was either a helpless blonde to be saved or a whiny brunette to be brought along for the ride. The only media more heterocentric was the kind from each preceding generation, each featuring a slick, straight, white male saving the day.

This was the norm, as it has been from most myths, religions, and tribal tales since the first conquering village shared ale around a fire pit. And it's just part of the dominant species' wiring. It doesn't mean it's right, it just means it's dominant. But the big, bad, dumb boys movies still do the best. Especially the ones with the cars and the exploding things.

At my core—brain, gut, chemicals—I'm not just a heterocentric lump or simply predisposed to a flurry of thoughts and characteristics found in every culture since the first men created the first club without wives. I am—you are too, of course—so much more than the sum of our predispositions. But, if those predispositions are there, we must learn how to use them and react to them outside of a dominant historical narrative, while still maintaining that our point of view is the only one we can reason ourselves into.

And if you're going to Hooters or the beach, I'll sit this one out.

Jesus Doesn't Text and the Buddha Hasn't Tweeted Yet

"BETWEEN THE POPE AND AIR CONDITIONING," says Harry Block of Woody Allen's 1997 *Deconstructing Harry*, "I'd choose air conditioning."

The Pope, however, *does* have a castle. And cool outfits.

But the sentiment of that quote, that in our modern age an individual would choose science, technology, and convenience over mythology (and the anxiety that comes with belief) —remains appropriate, especially in this modern age where "Nones" and "Dones" (non-religious and "done with" religion adults) are growing in numbers while the faithful are seeing declines like never before.

In a world full of air conditioning, bottled water, Pop Tarts, seedless watermelons, and endless computers in the hands of children, it's easy for nonbelievers to rely on modern convenience and leave the possessions, miracles, and conversions to badly produced religious movies (and some well-produced Hollywood films) and tall tales, where they belong. There are no miracles, there is no Devil, and most parents will choose medicine over straight "prayer-changes-things" sessions any day.

We're awash in a non-religious reality, the whole Western world over.

What if there really was a new Buddha?

Enter "Buddha Boy," otherwise known as Ram Bahadur Bomjon, Nepal's breakout religious star who, since 2005, has drawn followers, admirers, and skeptics for his meditative practices and belief that he is a reincarnation of the "real" Buddha. This is the same Buddha Boy who caught *my* attention and potential belief in 2006 when, almost a decade into my atheism, I thought *this could be the real thing*. This could be it—a real, magical being who actually does something to prove there is more to this temporal plane of existence. History is dubious concerning all of the saints, prophets, saviors, and such—but a real, live miracle worker! Here in the flesh!

I *also* thought—which is usually my first thought about these things—that it was and is a hoax and will pass; but the part of me that holds out hope for the miraculous temporarily blinded the skeptical, realistic part of me that checks my passion and enthusiasm on a daily basis. If the Buddha Boy had powers to meditate, heal, and transcend physical existence, then all bets were off. I'd have to give magic and belief another chance. I'd give trying to believe in God another chance. I might have even have thought about the arduous road back to being some sort of religious person, which was someone I had stopped being.

But wait a minute—just because you can meditate under a tree doesn't mean that you can heal or that reincarnation is real. There are more logical fallacies in the want and practice of belief than in anything else. We do it all the time. We *want* to believe so we construct scaffolds that aren't there in order to prop up presuppositions that aren't there, in order to make things true because we want them to be true. Plus, I've seen more than enough "Magic's Biggest Secrets" videos to know that—sorry, Harry Potter and My Little Bronies—there is no real magic.

And if you're a real student of Buddhism, Christianity, or any myth, then you know that there are plenty of prophets and saints who exist to simply point the way to "the Truth" rather than acting as "the Truth." "Be your own light," the Buddha supposedly said in his last sermon. Which Buddha? Good question. There have been many.

And Buddha Boy? Just like my almost-episode of belief, he disappeared soon after making headlines, only to return to the public spotlight in 2014, without an official Facebook,

Twitter*, or Instagram. You'd think the Buddha today would be able to spread his message of peace way easier than any of the Buddhas of old.

I just *can't* believe

The thing is, I *can't* believe. It's just not in me. I want to. I once did. I see the value in it. But it just doesn't make *total* sense — any of it, not one religion, cult, or myth. Belief in religion is a bank I can't trust and a person I can't fall in love with. And I've tried, time and again, for years, in ways you probably haven't if belief has come easy to you, which it does for many people.

Science, history, and logic all convene on this point: miracles don't actually happen, prayer doesn't change things directly (or measurably), and no one has ever risen from the dead or emitted magical powers for real.

And *nobody* can go months without food or water while meditating, unless they have a friend or priest feeding them food through a false wood panel backing every night, or some sort of trickery. The "real" Buddha was said to have existed on one grain of rice a day. I don't believe that either, because it's also said that he exited the womb walking, preaching, and with a full set of teeth.

But I was hoping.

Who's your yogi?

The problem with Buddhas, saviors, and prophets is that they're all the same, and their followers always believe that they're *not* always the same. Always.

Whether you're rooting for Jesus Christ, Joseph Smith, L. Ron Hubbard, Buddha Boy, or the latest self-help guru (or an "actual" guru), all cult leaders and religious figures say and ask for the same thing: denial of your family and friends who won't believe, full acceptance of faith (which, believers come to believe, is actually "sight" and not belief), and trust that there is only one way, which you happen to be part of. And if anyone says differently, they're just persecuting you with their criticism. It's foolproof! And the oldest game out there.

But I *wanted* to believe, and for a brief while I was hoping that this 15-year-old was the actual answer to the invented saviors of history. What I mean by that is that all of the icons and saviors have had poor records of proving the actualities of their existence, writing things down, and having proof of their appearances confirmed for the world at large to witness and accept. It's convenient that almost everyone in the world was illiterate until the last two hundred years, when humanity started its religious decline, and there are minimal examples of "miraculous" happenings today when it would behoove prophets and supernatural beings to have their own YouTube channels. What better way to convert the world than performing the miracle of the loaves and fishes on Snapchat or Vine?

You see, any time a psychic, faith-healer, medium, priest, prophet, religious icon, or zealot claims superpowers or extra-human abilities, they must be tested. Today this would be easy—we have science laboratories and video-analysis software. The past million years? Not so much.

Growing up, I remember receiving mail from television evangelists that encouraged you to simply plant special dirt and seeds, or pray with your hand on the outline of a hand on the mail package. Even as a child I thought, *if this were true, wouldn't the whole world want a piece?*

If it were true. Because none of it is. But we all wish it was.

"*the_buddha1 hasn't tweeted yet"

Time will tell. The Buddha Boy, who is now in his mid-twenties, might just turn out to be the first real prophet with superhuman abilities, who proves that reincarnation, telepathy, mind-over-matter, and a spiritual plane of existence are as real as the parts of the book and video store that also claim they are. Religion, History, and Nonfiction are sorted separately.

Messages of world-wide peace are nothing new; international figures brokering diplomatic deals are nothing new; potential Earthly saviors are nothing new—but a real person embodying these elements, walking among us—*that* is something that history has never actually confirmed, although historians have been cajoled into "confirming" the "facts" of religion from time to time. If he—or she—walked among us, I might just become a follower, maybe just on Twitter.

Either way, I'll be waiting, patiently, like the Buddha.

Do they have air conditioning in Nepal?

Not to Be Read Before Halloween: 9 Ways We Can Truly (Truly, Truly!) Save Christmas (Once and for All)

EVERYONE KNOWS THAT EVERY YEAR, the minute that the last bag of Halloween candy is marked down at your local Buy n' Bag, the red and green go up, and with it the silly season of savings for the holiday that saves.

So of course, everyone also knows that every year the very same holiday needs saving from the ne'er-do-wells that would do it harm!

So here we go, ace! Here are some real world, multi-partisan, trans-denominational, hyper-humanistic suggestions and quick fixes that would ameliorate, alter, and save the greatest retail seasonal day ever (while possibly generating a cavalcade of new traditions and TV specials).

1. Move Christmas to February

Jesus can share his birthday with Lincoln and Washington, and we can extend the holiday cheer two more months throughout the bleak midwinter. This way we all stave off the post-New-Years-when's-the-next-holiday blues. This will also give us two extra months for savings! And between the new Presidents/Christmas holiday and spring, it's only like eight weeks! We could keep the Christmas/Winter break vacation AND keep Presidents' week vacation as well. Win-win.

2. Forget the gifts

I would LOVE Christmas if it was like Thanksgiving—family getting together to eat and drink then eat pie. That's it. No gifts, no stress over being "thoughtful" for the people in your life. Don't get me wrong—I love being thoughtful. I just can't be thoughtful about everyone in my life all at once while rushing through the mall, hoping that my $15 gift bought at the last minute is special enough to warm the heart of someone who already loves me. I just can't do it. Maybe if it were one gift per person, either homemade, drinkable, or something they specifically told me they needed. Moonshine would cover all of those categories.

Ok, you're getting moonshine. All of you.

3. Let's start a new holiday that will actually save the world

I will call it "New Xmas" and instead of getting gifts for people we know, we will ONLY get gifts for strangers in need. Everyone will be assigned a homeless shelter, family and school in need, and forest to help (you know, buying a tree to put back in the ground rather than the regular Christmas tradition of throwing away non-recyclable paper as soon as you rip it off the plastic-wrapped gift).

So whatever you were planning on spending on regular Christmas, you could spend on New Xmas. This could all be done anonymously for various reasons. No tax breaks, assholes. And if you wanted to help a family in another way other than gifts, so be it (helping someone find a place to live or a job or goods). "X" would mark the spot for true savings.

Let's save each other, shall we? We have enough to go around, right?

4. Reverse Christmas

Between Halloween and December 25th, we would spend as little as possible and only focus on getting out of debt. Then come December 25th we'd all meet at our favorite stores and buy something (just something small and nice) only for ourselves (and maybe finally order that sushi boat for dinner that we've been thinking about getting for years now).

5. HalloweenMas

We combine Halloween and Christmas, and on the big day (date pending), you get tricked or treated based on your outfit (and possibly your good deeds for the year), which you have spent all Fall and early Winter preparing for the big day. Each neighborhood will get a list of possible gifts to purchase for whomever shows up at your door, and you get to give said gift if you decide that the costume on the neighbor at your door is worthy of it. If not, then you get to keep the gift and "trick" the neighbor at your door by stating "maybe next year" and then shutting the door.

Good luck with borrowing their snow blower come January.

6. Animal Christmas

We all adopt unwanted animals as our one gift and/or go vegan for the Christmas season. At the end of the season you can go back to omnivorism but you have to keep the adopted pet(s). If you don't want a new pet or to go vegan, then you can celebrate by focusing on another helpless and domesticated population of your choice.

7. The All-In-UU-Santa-nalia-MythMas

…as in we rewrite the "Christmas" story to represent all (and I mean all) the "Christmas" and "holiday" stories including made-up stories featuring magical babies, reindeer, misfit toys, and latest YouTube and Meme trend-Christmas-tie-ins. This would combine all of history's myths, religions, traditions, and current saccharin cultural tales tied into this magical season.

All of them. Get ready for the true tale of a baby elf born on a foreign planet sent to Earth to teach us what giving or retail is all about, and so forth. This could get interesting. Doctor Who Christmas specials would have to take the lead on this one, as they are the one true guide of all-inclusive Christmas specials. And yes, Virginia, *Die Hard* is a Christmas movie, so get ready for the mythos to expand all kinds of different ways from gritty-cop Sunday.

8. Just make it a Winter thing

More than half of the "Christmas" and "holiday" songs are about Winter and food and family and making out, so let's cut the facade and make Christmas just a Winter thing, or at least keep playing the Wintery Christmas songs until late January.

Lights, songs, warmth—these are winter themes, not Christmas themes, right? Evergreen trees are popular in winter because, well, almost all the other plant life is dead. So All-Winter-Solstice-Mas it is. Or something catchier. Someone tell Sufjan Stevens, as he will be our official first artist in residence.

9. Get rid of Christmas altogether

Let's face it: the people who really really really celebrate the real reason for the season are the true non-gift-crazy Puritans who celebrate baby Jesus and grown up Jesus whenever they can. They don't need Santa to help with their cause. The rest of us are celebrating a made-up day when we buy that one big gift—and a sprinkling of other gifts—we'd probably save for a birthday or, you know, never. It's a holiday that demands that if purchasing was spread evenly over the whole year, and we liked seeing our family more, retail wouldn't need the get-in-the-black Friday to even out sales and "save" businesses (including Mobil and McDonald's who love our travel holidays).

Just go see your family or buy someone something nice every now and then, or don't. No need for the big narrative and soundtrack behind it.

Now pass the pie and moonshine. It's time for a holiday.

It's Literally All in His Head: A Year of Migraines and the Transparent Eyeball

IT WAS THE DAMN VIDEO GAME on the big screen that did me in.

There I was at our favorite superstore, staring at Mario Kart as my son played, and my vertigo kicked in. It was all those karts and colors and fast moving things.

The vertigo I had suffered from the previous year—viral vertigo, as fate would have it, brought on by stress or a virus—hadn't affected me for months, and there I was, in the middle of Target, wanting to lie down and make the world stop spinning.

I made it to the car and, after loading the kids in and asking the wife to drive, lost my balance and took a hard spill, whacking my head against the doorframe of the family wagon.

And that was it.

Hello concussion. Hello migraines. Hello new, awful world of brain pain.

The day was the Ides of March, and, being an English teacher, the possible irony wasn't lost on me—I had not been aware of senators lurking in the patio furniture section or treasonous opportunists in the dollar aisle. I am no Caesar.

My banishment to live as a walking sweatshirt

It wasn't my first concussion, but it will hopefully be my last. I had suffered minor concussions and whiplash before but never this awful level of brain pain, mental fog, and nausea. That sickening wash over your body from the skull to the neurons in your feet; the want to cry because you realize you've bruised your brain (and the fact that you are a brain, and a brain is all you have because it makes everything work);

and the stress and anxiety over ever extra strain and pressure from readjusting to daily life.

It was all part of a package I hadn't asked for, but was now mine. My eyes wouldn't stop flittering, and my face bones hurt.

I began a new journey, at home, for weeks as a walking sweatshirt. Me—a tall teacher, coach, and dad, reduced to sleeping undercovers all day, and hiding from the lights and sounds that made the pressure and headaches worse, missing out on time with my wife and children, and feeling like I had been given a new body that no one should inherit.

All I could do was pull my hood and cap over my eyes and sleep with minimal light. My eyeballs hurt. My forehead ached. The spot above my right ear where I hit my head hurt for months.

Months.

And your new life-long friend is…the migraine

Headaches had never been a thing for me—I have suffered here and there from a host of ills: broken bones, mononucleosis, back problems, tendonitis, IBS, colitis, gastritis, anemia, pneumonia, ear infections, hernias, depression, anxiety, and stress. Doctors love me.

Vertigo had been my newest diagnosis until the concussion, and one that my neurologist said would also be my friend for life.

I had never really suffered from a headache, however. Toothaches, belly aches, back and shoulder pain, yes. But headaches were never my thing.

Certain anti-inflammatory drugs I knew very well, but I would begin the round robin tournament featuring several doctors, various types of drugs, and my central nervous system that would like, reject, or overly object to pills that often "would take a few weeks to build up in your system" or cause dizziness and nausea while offering to cure dizziness and nausea.

This lasted for months (and is ongoing, even a year after), and the greatest remedy is a low-stress, low-light, and low sound environment. However, my life is full of sound, light, and screen.

Friends, students, and strangers confided in me, secretly, of their similar plights, and the drugs and remedies that worked for them, some who had suffered multiple concussions, migraines, and had spent between months and years recovering.

Years recovering? When I first felt that bottomless pit of brain drudgery, as if my shoulders were melting into my shoes and my head was an ice brick slowly being crushed, I figured I would recover in two days—maybe a week—and be back to work, performing for my English Language Arts students.

Constant noise, light, and action in the classroom and hallway would prove to be dangerous obstacles, as would standing upright without feeling dizzy or nauseated. And–this is a fun fact–my loud, booming voice gives me headaches. My own voice.

As a coach I feared the soccer balls that my talented student-athletes would kick at 90 miles per hour, or the rough play on the field somehow taking me down with it.

Any time I dinged my head against a wall, even ever-so-gently, I spiraled into hours and even days of headachery.

When my children would jump on my back and slightly hit my head by accident, it would send visible ripples through my dome. I made sure my eight and six-year-old reminded me every time that I went into the basement I had to be careful not to hit my head. My wife knew the damage I had done to my head before the major concussion when she would hear a loud thump of the pipes in the basement, followed by loud cursing and me ascending the stairs rubbing my head.

I felt like a house of cards, ready for the wind to take me.

Feeling wounded, weak, and inside-out

After the concussion I felt like I was destined to live in fear of the next blunt force trauma to the head. It was part caution, part paranoia, and part familiar trope. The thought haunted me and crept in my daily life—and still does. My internal current shifted, and my inner colors tinted to a new shade and hue.

When you have such pain in your head that you can't open your eyes, you tend to feel that the next logical step is to shut down and enter a final rest.

With the concussion and subsequent migraines that followed, I was a wounded animal, feeling helpless and fearful that one more hit to the noggin could spell untimely doom. And these feelings are hard to shake when you're living inside the head that is constantly processing the pain inside your head. At least broken bones, an upset stomach, and back pain are ills you can have while still being able to think without being interrupted by a headache.

But when your brain is swelling and inflamed all the time, rational thinking seeps out of the ear and into the bed sheets or couch.

I think of the poet and Transcendentalist philosopher Ralph Waldo Emerson calling himself a "transparent eyeball" while observing nature: I was a brain, thinking with my brain, observing my brain as my brain hurt. All bodily functions and my entire thought life operated through the same damaged thing I was trying not to injure anymore.

Feelings, thoughts, fear, dreams, all of it: they come from the brain, which I felt trapped inside of.

You only get one brain, and that's it. You shouldn't knock it around.

Screens, screens, all types of screens

Ne'er pull your hat upon your brows/Give sorrow words. The grief that does not speak/Whispers the o'er fraught heart and bids it break. –Macbeth, 4.3

Students came to my aid when I returned to work—two of them who had recently gotten over concussions. "Hey Mr. McKeen, no more screen time for you," they'd say, in a caring way, along with checking up on me throughout each week. They knew. Concussions were serious, and people with them needed time and a quiet space to heal.

I wasn't talkative with many people at work about my concussion and migraines because I had never been wounded like this before, and when people sense weakness, they take advantage and assume you're down for the count (even though I work with wonderful teachers who are compassionate, empathetic, and extremely giving). My spirit had altered itself to be a protective force–I was more anxious than ever, as my brain had taken on new fears and characteristics that my general extroverted nature wasn't used to.

In the first months after the concussion, I lost words as I typed and thought, and felt myself thinking slower. I would lose my place more often while lecturing and quickly recover, but the change was apparent to me, if not to my students.

I'm not a crier, but I felt that anger and frustration that makes you want to cry, and still feel it. Sometimes it's as if my tear ducts dry heave, grieving for the loss of old friends who had been lodged inside my grey matter.

My neurologist suggested working a half-day schedule–I wish. My career doesn't exist in a world where you can work from home or take half-days, and two-thirds of my life are taken up in front of screens. If I wasn't writing on the smartboard at work, I was using a P.C. or laptop to write and create lesson plans. There was also the smartphone. And the TV. And the tablet. The world was all too much to stare at.

Good thing I love to read paperbacks.

Getting my life back, one cup of Bergamot at a time

When your brain is broken, you don't get a new one.

It's been a year since the concussion and the start of my daily struggle with headaches, head pressure, and full-on, awful parade-length migraines. Depending on the weather and amount of stress, I'm learning to manage trying to be the strong, productive citizen I've always tried to be, and the best husband, father, son, friend, and worker I can be.

Over the last twelve months I've gone days (and even weeks) without brain pain, thanks to the right balance of medication, sleep, and weather. I've also had weeks of touch-and-go headaches that didn't care what rest or pharmaceuticals I tried.

A year ago I thought I had escaped a concussion unharmed, and instead ended up starting an un-magical row of seasons where I literally took things a morning and a cup of tea at a time.

Hopefully one day I will be migraine-free and enjoy all the light, noise, and stress that life tries to offer. Until then, the lights will be turned low, I'll be simplifying things, and I might just need a little extra time to get my brain on the right page for whatever adventure might appear in the wonderful world that is daily life.

They're All Sex Maniacs!

LIKE MANY WELL-ADJUSTED ADULTS and parents, I grew up in the church—*well* "churched," that is—from Vacation Bible School and youth group every Friday night to Bible Studies, prayer groups, and more than one service on Sunday.

And with that, I—along with millions of others across many religions and religious purity cultures—came to view my "fearfully and wonderfully made" body and the bodies of others as not only *sinful and* the cause of God's justified hatred of sin, but that our bodies are not our own but rather "belong" to God and patriarchal cultures.

What an awful way to think about bodies, sex, and culture.

And what an awful way to raise children responsibly.

If I knew then what I know now, I'd have to share the following with my then-teenage self who didn't know anything about sex, gender, babies, love, marriage, divorce, or relationships.

You are not just a sinful meatbag with sexy parts.

You're not.

You're just not.

Yes, you have a biological determination within your genes and sexual organs that draws you to create life with other people during sexual intercourse (or not if you're asexual, gay, or choose not to).

But just like your whole life is not based on what you smell with your nose or write with your hand, you should not live in fear that your whole life will be judged on who you kiss, cuddle, hold hands with, or have sexual relations with.

There are greater things to judge your life on—or not. It's not all about judgment, it's about living right and being mentally stable and existentially kind and aware.

You're going to have lots of sex with possibly more than one person.

You're going to live a long time—and possibly have more than three or ten sexual partners and/or spouses or long time significant others.

You just are. It's how humans are.

And that's okay.

Most of you women will outlive your male husbands by ten to twenty years, and most of you will get divorced more than once, or break up with someone you thought you would be with forever.

That's just data.

And within or without the confines of marriage, you are going to have lots and lots of sex in different positions and ways, whether you share that publicly or not, and whether it's "nice, simple married sex" or not (and I would also assert that neither God nor the angels are watching this or taking notes).

You are not responsible for unwanted stares or sexual advances.

Your bare shoulders, thighs, legs, midriff, calves, ankles, hair, or wrists are yours to show off or not, based on your profession, values, or sense of self and personality.

You are not responsible for the sexual abuse or harassment done against you, nor are you responsible for the thoughtcrime of "sin" done by someone else because they like, lust after, or love you.

You may not be just heterosexual.

You might be gay, bisexual, pansexual, asexual, or "other," and that's okay as long as you're being safe, kind, and legal.

And you might just be heterosexual.

You ARE "wonderfully made"

You are the result of millions of years of evolution, survival, specific choices, and modern technical and scientific advancements that have made you healthy and alive (and that billions of life forms haven't had the chance to enjoy).

You have sexual organs and nerve endings which feel amazing when stimulated.

You have the amazing ability to create and carry life, whether you're making 85 million sperm a day or carrying up to 1,000 eggs with you since before birth.

Wow.

You are more than the sum of your parts.

Men—you are not God's chosen dominant half of the species.

Women—you are not subservient to men in any sense of the societally prescribed way.

Equal is equal when we talk about the roles of men and women, and although we are sexual creatures, we are far from being just sexual or biological creatures.

And if you stay "pure" until marriage—which may be your choice—there is no way to quantify "purity" in terms of a lasting marriage, happiness, daily life, or God's judgment.

So live without fear!

And be safe out there.

13 Ways We Can All Achieve Total Perspective

AS THE SOMEWHAT OBVIOUS yet profound saying goes about perspective, it really *does* all depend on how you look at it.

Wherever you are in life, there is some struggle or suffering that you're going through or about to go through. Somehow it's always inevitable whether you're a student, parent, young individual, or fledgling professional (or anyone in-between). But if you're prepared with the right set of eyes (and most of us aren't), then you'll be able to tackle any setback, obstacle, or low point, all in good time.

So forget trying to achieve Maslow's highest level of Self-Actualization. Forget trying to be perfect. You can even forget trying to fulfill your true potential, if just for a while. And you can even stop forgetting *forgetting*, as the Yogis and Jedis teach. What you might need is sharp, willful perspective, and a heavy dose of reality to get you to where you should be (and maybe where you want to be). Here's how.

1. Start with your deathbed and work backwards
There are three ultimate and undeniable realities: Death, Nature, and the Unknown.

The sooner you realize you're incapable of controlling these three, the sooner you'll feel a little release from Life's cool grip. As you are dying a long time from now, who will you be surrounded by and what will your final wish be? What will you have let go of? If you can imagine your life from your final moment backwards to right now, then you'll have constructed enough timelines to know what you really want (which might not be what you think you want). This isn't meant to make you meditate on your own death, but rather to jostle you out of the current moment and consider the long arc of your life.

2. You're going to get old (and be old) for a while

Consider this: between your twenties and retirement, you will live almost three lifetimes as you did between birth and the age of twenty. And then you're going to have a brand new life in retirement. Most men die around seventy-six, and most women out-live men by ten to fifteen years (often twenty). Those nice, old church ladies? They're living a second and third life after career and children, many of them in retirement and then widowed. Life is long and you're going to have time, so prepare for early mornings and long afternoons, and plenty of time to look back to now and wish you knew what to change—and change it while you're young. That should take some of the pressure off, but know that the dreams you're not getting around to right now might be waiting for you on the other side of life, when the world will still belong to the young, fast ones.

3. It's not about the salary (unless it's about the salary)

In business and life, there is only the job. Or rather—there should only *be* the job, in that too often we love the pomp and circumstance of it all, long after the usefulness of the title has disappeared. If you strip away the celebration about the worker, and you focus one's skill set on simply getting the job done to perfection, then that's all that should matter. However, humanity has never been good at ego-less work, and yet we keep creating fictional heroes whose main focus is "the job" when in reality we have entire industries on building things that will be obsolete by the time Junior finishes high school. So for you select few who are out there creating a solid product no matter what, you're the ones holding it together in terms of perspective.

4. Think like a lawyer (for both sides)

Find that angle on human behavior and look to defend the possibly indefensible because it will open up new avenues of thought as to who we are and what we are capable of. Lawyers exist because everyone needs a friend and defender at some point (even if you lose and have to pay them). But, like odd priests, they debate the law in ever advancing and illuminating ways. Did you ever think that discussion of logic could continue forever? Law school students did. The minute we make villains of people is the minute we shut down the possibility that a person is a person, and not a predestined character. Somewhere between one side's truth and the other side's defense is the reality we're going to settle for. And sometimes we all just need a good arbiter.

5. Think like a doctor—medical, academic, scientific, or witch variety

Everything can be diagnosed, and for all things there is an answer. There, doesn't that make you feel better? Once we have a diagnosis we can let the fear and stress of the Unknown go and we can move onto the next thing. The sooner you accept that we're all walking head cases with our own family and chemical issues, the sooner you'll feel an opening in your mind as to the right kind of compassion you could be showing your nearest stranger, friend, or family member. There are years of layers, conflicts, and stories going on in every person you meet, and we are often unaware of what we're being guided by. Sometimes you need an ambulance, and sometimes you just need a tall glass of water.

6. Respect the sweaty man (and woman)

Right now there are literally millions of people sweating more than you at jobs harder than yours and in situations tougher than yours. There's someone older and more prone to aches than you are in fields, caves, and factories all over the globe. The inverse is true as well. The dream for all of us, however, is to be able to reap some reward from that sweat and then be able to relax with our loved ones on a couch at the end of the day (preferably with a cold beverage, a hot meal, and syndicated reruns). That's all of humanity. All of it. And it's a good dream. In fact, it's all there ever has been, going back to the first species that hurried home from work to watch the sun set. We're all connected to that end-of-the-day dream and the sweaty reality before us.

7. Make 'em laugh, make 'em laugh, make 'em laugh

Comedians have all the answers. With the right amount of skepticism, empathy, and self-deprecation, you can laugh your way around a problem just by observing the absurd nature of most situations. But chances are that most of us see things in terms of function or emotion rather than humor. The mind of a comic is ever-racing for that quip or laugh no matter what, and it's a true art to master. Almost anything can be funny in the right context, and in comedy we have all of literature, myth, and art with sharp commentary and philosophy. There are often more metaphors, analogies, and proverbs in a comedy routine than you'd expect.

8. Consider the Other…and the Other, and the Other

"The Other" is just that – he or she who is not one of us, a foreigner, an outsider, an *other*. There is nothing like a good old fashioned clique to ruin every institution since the dawn of mankind, and you must accept the possibility that all humans need consideration, especially the ones you're not considering. Right now there is a version of you in every country around the world, and the same goes for humans going back in time to the beginning of bipedal experimentation. Our worst times as a species has been when we thought we were the only ones who mattered for whatever special reasons we told ourselves.

9. Count your blessings at least three times—or four

If you haven't realized how good you have it lately, just think about how luxurious it is to sit on an indoor toilet while watching your Smartphone, and that most of the world doesn't have access to clean running water, let alone Smartphones, WiFi, indoor plumbing, and endless aisles of discounted toilet paper in giant food stores. Go ahead, count all your blessings. We'll wait.

10. You're probably wrong about a number of things—beware the Fallacies!

If we let our irrationality go unchecked, and we have enough people telling us we're fine just the way we are, we're lucky enough to spend a whole lifetime of never being challenged out of our daily mental narratives. That's when our personal relationships and professional lives suffer. In your mental routine, allow for the possibility that you're wrong about what you're doing, or that you have the wrong premise. Or that the system (job, relationship, group) has some flaw that, if corrected, could improve everything immensely. There have been whole nations and empires built on the wrong premises, and they were still filled with well adjusted people who lead lives of happy mediums – and plenty who suffered at the hands of unchecked power.

11. Just ask "why" three times on three different levels—and then listen

There is always a "root" to the root of the problem, and usually the solutions can't be far off (although, sometimes they are). But if you really want to get your Ego out of the way on a decision, and you want your subconscious and unconscious to unite in the most powerful way possible, then you have to keep asking *why* until you get the right answer.

You have to disarm yourself, if possible. Sometimes when you're listening, there is no audible *yes* or *no*, so you have to just go with it. If you jump, you might have to build the net on your way down. Why? Because life is dangerous and full of the unknown. Why? Because that is the nature of existence.

Why? Well, you see how it goes from here. Include clarifying questions, qualifiers, and the hard, direct questions you don't necessarily *want* to answer. It's worth it.

12. When in doubt, take a shower

Practicing mindfulness while meditating in nature is preferable, but there's nothing like a hot shower and some alone time to get you thinking and maybe clear your mind. The billions of microbes all over your body need some perspective, too.

13. You're the hero we've been waiting for—but you're not the only hero

Every person is the main protagonist in a stand-alone narrative, regardless of how we characterize each other as a sidekick, enemy, comic relief, or extra. And we're all on a revolving cycle of importance whether we're new to the storyline or the old character looking for a reboot. You are extremely important in every way possible to those who count on you—and the same goes for everyone else. Take great care with your storyline because it will end someday, and those who have shared the pages with you will be better for it.

Hugs, Drugs, and Mugs of Coffee — How to College Properly

"YOU'RE ABOUT TO BE BORN," I tell my seniors long before their high school graduation day.

"So far we've coddled you and kept you in diapers. Now some of you have already started living, and some of you haven't. But you're all about to be born."

It confuses some of them until they're about 19 or 20, but then it makes sense.

Some of them even get it within the first two weeks of summer after their last graduation party.

I don't remember any advice about life from anyone for the "reality" of post-high school existence after graduation — not even from our high school graduation speaker (who, I will bet, like any graduation speaker, is never listened to by anyone except for a few bored teachers in the audience).

I entered the summer of my life after high school a blank slate, ready for college, life elsewhere, and whatever life would throw at me.

I did okay. But here's what I wish someone had told me so I could forget and figure it all out for myself.

Don't fall in love with your first foot rub.
Ah, those magical orientation days of college. Fresh faces from around the world, day trips wearing matching t-shirts, and bus rides with the best and brightest.

And the girls. Oh, the college girls.

It was on the way back from a freshmen Boston trip that a certain someone who seemed totally out of my league let me rub her feet for some reason—and I was more than willing to capture her favor.

But it ended badly, months later, after I had spent my first six weeks or so chasing her (and catching her a few times) with a wide-eyed crushed heart. She was worth it, I guess, but if I was able to tell that young me not to rush into things, I might have.

Ah hell, he wouldn't have listened.

Yes, you are in competition with everyone else.

If you get one of those "look to your left, now look to your right—only one of you will make it to sophomore year" speeches from the dean, peer mentors, or the orientation crew, they're *right*.

Most of you are going to drop out, lose your scholarships, transfer, take time off and never go back, take time off and go back in a few semesters or years, and/or finish online. And that's fine.

But for institutions full of the best of the best of the best of the best, college isn't just full of the best. Some of the best can't afford it, and the rest of the best are in trade schools, the military, the work force, or waiting to finish up those expensive required classes at community, online, or state college before transferring.

Only 30-40 percent of freshmen become seniors in four years, and less than that finish in six years.

It is what it is, without my judgment—but that magical feeling you have during your first semester might just go away by Christmas.

I was lucky and finished in four years—but not all of my freshmen friends did, and some of my best friends never finished at all—even 20 years later—or are still finishing college credits.

Stay healthy, stay healthy, stay healthy!

If you can avoid pregnancy, STIs, mononucleosis, drug and alcohol abuse and/or addiction, chronic fatigue, easily communicable diseases, homesickness, brokenheartedness, stress, anxiety, depression, and a bevy of other strange things that you may catch or pass on while living with thousands of other people, good on you.

But for the rest of us, plan ahead, use protection and preventative measures, and be prepared to get sick and make that midnight CVS run—or a few of them.

And don't wait to get treatment, whether it's for what you think is just more than a cold or something like counseling, which will improve your health and wellbeing the most.

Sometimes you'll need rest and water, and sometimes you'll need an ambulance.

Go to bed. Now.

College means non-stop parties, new friends and interests who want to stay up and watch the sunrise, and late night cram sessions on top of all-nighters (yes, there are different categories of each). So choose your fun wisely, and make sure it is sprinkled around library and bookstore study time.

Study now and play later. Don't let the "new Friday night" become every night.

Chances are you're going to miss out on something, and that's all right. Hopefully it won't be a $60K education.

Don't be the idiot who trained for this his whole life and had to drop out right away.

However you want to take that, take it. Some kids burn out right away and some kids fall into the wrong set of addictions. And usually these kids have been training for college since pre-K.

There will be shame and embarrassment among family and friends if you flunk out of college after years of middle and high school honors and AP classes and stringent athletic, theatre, arts, music, and academic discipline.

But it will be okay. You're only a teenager. You're allowed a few screw-ups in life.

There are more than a few paths to success in life, and eventually you won't just be that idiot who trained for this for their whole life and had to drop out. There are many roads to redemption, and failing at something when you're eighteen is okay. Really. It's okay.

College is a magical place where the future happens.
It's true. College was once something only for the richest and most privileged males who would join networks of other successful and privileged males, and the rest of us would have to work in their factories and build their railroads and knick-knacks.

But not anymore. College opened up to everyone and was once affordable, and then slowly became unaffordable. But now, thanks to online learning and progressive politicians, colleges and universities are becoming less insanely overpriced for the working family, and are still a place of excellent networks for professionals.

And living with like-minded, talented, highly intelligent, and determined people is a magical thing, even though it's one of the hardest journeys known to humanity (until marriage, parenting, the professional workforce, your first company, and graduate, medical, or law school). You might even (like most people) meet your lifelong friends there, and become who you truly were born to be.

And about that foot rub…
Cliches to avoid in love and lust while finding your way as a developing eighteen or nineteen-year-old (or an older, bearded transfer student):

-thinking you need a romantic partner to feel complete or achieve the "college" experience

-dating the best friend of the one who is really in love with you

-hooking up with random partygoers just to "get ahead" (or to get head) in terms of your reputation

-trading going to class and studying for hooking up and/or the bar (or bong, or sleep)

-falling in love too quickly

-not falling in love quickly enough

-avoiding a real relationship because of fear or embarrassment

-trapping yourself in damaging stereotypes because it's all you've known

-pursuing others when you should be focusing on yourself

-taking others for granted because you're young and invincible

-being too young to take any of this advice (the greatest cliche of all!)

All the best to you, younguns!

    Now get to class and if the professor isn't there in 12 minutes, I'll see you on the quad.

I Was the Seventh Black Kid on the Bus

I HAVE A SOMEWHAT DRY JOKE to explain a bit of my history from my high school days, that I was the "seventh black kid on the bus."

That is, unlike the upper and upper-*upper*-class students who went to my prestigious Princeton preparatory high school, I was "bussed in from the city," which is usually code for a minority student or a person of color, which I'm not.

And to be fair to the joke, the bus usually only held maybe seven students—that's six black kids from my city only a few neighborhoods away, with whom I would wait for an extra hour after school while most other kids got rides in cars—and me.

I experienced this kind of ratio on and off growing up on the literal outskirts of the city—my neighborhood was the last part of Trenton before you entered the highway toward whiter cities, and down the street from the beautiful old houses that had become boarded up and abandoned from "white flight" or otherwise. If you took a picture of attractive row houses from the 50s and 60s, and aged them poorly, you'd get the long and winding West State Street, full of vibrant people living amidst worn down America.

I have the pleasure of the strange identity of living in a city that claims its roots in all the members of my family on both sides, full of history and racial divisions and bus routes. Trenton, like any other large city, was full of layered neighborhoods in varying shades of monied districts. There's the hospital where my grandmother worked; there's the tennis court my cousins and I play on; there is the old zoo without bears like they used to have; along *this* bus route are the schools and college my parents went to—all Trenton, all solid, all charmed wraps around my most recent family.

Growing up, my best friends were black and white and mixed, unlike the best friends of my parents and grandparents when they were young—all happenstance based on what neighborhood housed which kid. By middle school I would start a new school in Princeton, and learn the new bus and car routes that took me through richer and more monied roads, and into a circle of personal and educational excellence, at least that's what the expectation is (and probably should be) when you're paying top dollar.

That dangerous and mundane term, "white flight," that was synonymous with post-WWII cities had claimed Trenton years ago, when factories stopped providing jobs and the Levittowns started swallowing whole generations of white people whole. Thus went the shops and markets and schools, forcing parents to consider moving out (or just using grandma's address for school purposes), *choicing* out to "better" schools, or competing for the endless rows of private schools just down Route 206. And there were plenty, from Catholic to Old Money to New Preppy.

And there I was, on the outskirts, white faced, somewhat privileged, and unaware that America never really stopped fighting the Civil War nor did it complete the marches of the Civil Rights movement.

The white liberals up north had done what white liberals up north do, and the inverse about those in the South was the same.

And I proudly attended my prep school, only there because of scholarship and the sweat of my parents' brows to pay a fraction of what most classmates paid. During the day mom and dad taught school themselves in surrounding cities, and at night they worked extra jobs so I would have the best education that money could buy.

And I did.

But only a *few* other black kids from Trenton did too.

The rest got the real, gritty *city* experience, synonymous with urban, black, ghetto, dropout, neglect, and forgotten.

Growing up, I enjoyed black culture and all-black events here and there and never thought twice about it, unless someone made an awkward remark, which was fine because, as most people are hesitant to mention, there are plenty of differences between black and white cultures, especially the churches, but only slight differences everywhere else.

People are just people, you know. Most of them ride the bus.

But the reality of being white and leaving an all-black baseball practice (where I was often Jamal or Jermaine, but never Jeremy), or being just one of the white people leaving an all-black church service, or constantly being a white kid in the midst of a truly mixed crowd, left its mark on me, in that I would leave one "black place" after an event was done, and end up in a whiter neighborhood for dinner and bedtime.

Down *down* the street from my house were the lower classes, you see. Guns, drugs, prostitution, many of the things people drive from outside the city to experience in the black of night.

In my neighborhood we had the lower-middle to slightly more middle class homes, but on the bus we traveled to a specific niche of a select circle of high schools, down the street from Princeton University and the pinnacle of American upper classes, literally *right across the street* from the Governor's Mansion and mansions that exceeded it in price, where I had classes with the children of upper class movers, shakers, and royalty from around the world.

And it was wonderful.

On that bus, in the morning, I studied for the extra hour I missed the night before, and on the way home I caught up with the day's events with my neighbors, the lot of us constantly aware that we were not of the city or neighborhood that taught and coached us.

And in that circle of kids was when I suspected, and then realized, and then, at some point, *knew* that, in the real world, no one would care that I had been the seventh "black kid" because I would step off that bus white, and go home white, and apply for jobs and colleges white.

Skin is the only thing you can't escape.

These days I'm a teacher in a city school where white kids are the minority, and my own children attend public school in a smaller, whiter town than I teach. Like all good parents, we strive to give our children the best possible life that we can afford—in energy, attention, and money—but still there is that sinking feeling that history has set apart the inner-cities for the lower classes and disenfranchised minorities among us, whether we're observing ancient towns as peace or the latest southside cities at war. That is, until the new hipster yuppies come and gentrify the hell out of it.

"Earning their place" in society has become the hackneyed go-to for explaining why it's okay to house certain people in the undesirable 'hoods while the few celebrate life a little better down the road. Life goes like that, right? The bottom levels are raised up, and new people come in to eventually rise too.

Except we all know that "earning your place" decades after emancipation, and then decades *more* after achieving equal rights, where a large section of a whole people is still as far away from "their place" as the generations were before them, is the highest-bought and sought-after fallacy.

My own privilege has its end in most parts of society, where class and accomplishment trumps every other characteristic, including my charm, articulation, and education. Unfortunately that privilege carries to most cities, and is celebrated by all the wrong people, who feel that because I was born a certain hue and was raised by similarly hued people, there is a higher meaning to my skin tone.

And here I thought we were all agreed that this was no longer a thing.

Somewhere in my junior year of high school I got a car, the greatest accomplishment for a young person.

This would end years of the bus winding through every road of the city, every 'hood and lower street, and every boarded up house and school on our way to the better promised land of upper-class living.

My morning driving would be this: make a left out of the driveway, get right on the highway, avoid the city, and end up in an entirely different grid of neighborhoods and businesses, all after four exits.

At some point before I achieved this independence from the bus and city-winding, I remember meeting the younger new kids from Trenton that would attend my high school—including the two new white kids who would take my place in the ratio of students who didn't pay full price for the privilege of higher education.

At that moment I felt more alive because having a car afforded me the greatest of human freedoms, and I no longer had to ride in the seatbelt-less green padded seats. Those two new kids from my city—and the others on the bus—would hopefully achieve freedom one day by way of car, and feel the independence and individualism that we were all promised in the beginning of every American History and American English textbook.

And I was no longer the white kid, or a kid at all—on the bus.

To My Brother, Who Is My Cousin -- a Plea for Family from an Only Child

TO MY *DEAR BROTHER*, MY OWN KIN, my side-by-side man, who is my cousin—I celebrate you, us, life itself, our mothers.

There is nothing else that can bind us more, and we have the entire expanse of life to explore. I have wanted you as my own brother, my friend, my secret sharer, and companion since we first met. To call you brother is the most natural thing I can think, and when I think of my life, I think of you. I count your years along with my own, and measure my life in step with yours—I am *this* many years, you are *this* many minus three. How old are you now? In line with my years. How is your health, wealth and happiness?

Measured along with the length of my reach to have you by my side until we grow old and share a seat at the diner down the street.

To my *dear sister*, my younger one, my half-twin, who is also my cousin—I celebrate the same, today, forever.

To call you sister is what I've always wanted; to be the older brother you can count on, and, along with your brother, be counted among the moments and movements of my life. This is my life, and there you are—part of me—and me, part of you. We are life itself and the tale humans have told since siblings walked tall among plains somewhere. Since day one you were the youngest, the last, the protected we somehow were sworn to shield. I count my blessings more than twice, and you are there, all along. My own.

Corner booth, same diner, the lot of us.

To my *foster brothers and sister* who are out there somewhere: you were my only siblings I ever had, if only for months (how *does* an only child have bunk beds?)—I have thought of you long upon these years, and we are almost reaching middle age and slowing down enough to find that it's time for some third act where we recount the years and missed connections, and parallel timelines, and wishes never granted.

To my *best men and friends*, who are also my chosen brothers in life, who have known me in my formative years, and shared the pangs of foolish maturation, I lay down my life for you easily, as we should.

There is no wedding or birthday complete without some revelry with you nearby—or there used to be, before we all moved away; there is no thought of my life without counting you and your babies, who share the same years with my children. Life has given us this one go-around, and it means everything that I could have you too. We shall grow old, cursing and blessing the Earth together as we share bourbon and song on porches as our children take our places in the great wide world. We shall sneak cigarettes behind the house and the wives will be no wiser, although the wives are often wiser.

And to my *brothers and sisters who died young*, whose caskets, memorials, and graves I have stood next to, wishing for more time, wishing to have known you better—you are with me in my drive to work, in the corners of rooms I sit alone in, and when I feel my age and my pinpoint in time. You are with me when I wish the world was set right. I am fortunate to have known you and to carry you in memory. I am never at a loss for words when I talk with you.

To my *brothers and sisters who have died at their own hands*—I know it wasn't my place to save you, but I wish it had been. I wish that life would have been boring instead of tumultuous, and lasted longer after the dark hours of suffering, and that you would have suffered enough here and there to push you beyond that one fateful day when you disappeared from the calendar. You are also with me in moments I walk alone, wishing you had chosen more and better hours. And I was almost one of you several times, swallowed up in darkness here and there also, and will never choose that now that I am older, and slower, and have decided that living is better than any other option, considering all options.

And to my *brothers fighting in a foreign land*, or taking up arms against one another; to those calling me brother, enemy, or something that mothers might be ashamed to hear: how I wish I could know you and your struggle, and we could see eye to eye on all the things that make us men, fathers, and sons.

How I wish those weapons could melt into shovels and we could build your family all the housing they need— someday, we sing.

Someday.

And I can't forget my *young sisters and brothers in the classroom* and shop floor and fields of play, those I've taught from their childhood and have seen become mothers and fathers and workers of the world. I count your lives sacred and singular, and consider your lives as part of my own, if only for a short while.

If I can hold this much family inside of my own arms, veins, and heart; fill up the years; and add your humanity to mine, then I will. It is a great and dangerous adventure, but life is long and full of time, and I will look for a word to call you, and it will be so.

Why All Men Hate the Beach

ALL MEN HATE THE BEACH, going to the beach, and the idea of a beach day.

Or maybe, all men hate sunbathing. Or maybe it's that all *dads* hate the beach. Ask any man (and we're talking men here, not teens or college-age boys or men who, fully clothed, like to walk their dogs at the beach after hours). I'm sure it's a mixture of all varieties of men, although I've seen men sunbathing here and there, and I just assumed that they fell asleep.

Why men beach it in the first place

Men go to the beach for two reasons: women and kids. Or to launch a kayak. And don't forget scuba classes. But almost no group of men will say to each other, "hey guys, want to sit, lay, and run around in the direct sun all day?" The answer is always that I already work in the hot, direct sun all day. I don't want to do it surrounded by sand. And old men in sunny beach-side cultures who fished for a living and spend their retirement days at the beach don't count. That's like hanging out near where you worked, which a lot of men do. In fact, legend has it that the first boat was invented when men were bored at the beach with their families and had to devise a way to break up the monotony of heating up and then taking a dip, heating up and then taking a dip, heating up and then taking a dip. You've all been there.

There's just something about being in the hot sun for hours without getting paid that makes men restless, resistant, and adverse to the lazy day at the beach. Don't get me wrong— I love doing nothing while my skin isn't burning and I'm showing signs of dehydration. Well, now that the kids are able to play on their own, I can do more of nothing at the beach, in the shade, guarding my stuff from the wiles of the desert sands.

Women LOVE the beach

On the other hand, women love the beach. Like, insanely love the beach. My working theory is that because our species' better half have monthly cycles like the moon, and the moon controls the waves, and women can control men best at the beach–women, therefore, love the beach. Maybe not all women, but at least 98 percent of them. Young women in bikinis can control men's actions, and older women in bikinis with offspring of those men can control men's actions. It's a vicious and beautiful cycle within a cycle within a cycle, all dependent on getting us men to the beach.

And for women there is some magical moment that happens when the sun hits the skin, something beyond a Vitamin D boost. Sunbathing or tanning is vital to a woman's happiness. Learn this, men. *Learn it, respect it, and never question it*. Any chance women can get to sunbathe, they will. This, dear men, allows you to be free to do other things but only if the kids are being watched. And when you bring men to the beach, they can play with the kids and you women are free to sunbathe. See? It's pure genius.

Before having kids, a beach trip might have been you and some friends, the wife, and a cooler of soda pop and sandwiches. Maybe you rode boogie boards ironically in your 20s or played frisbee. Maybe you showed up at the beach in jeans and a sweatshirt after hours for a BBQ or something youthful and curfew-free. But you weren't sitting or walking all day long in the hot sun unless that included said soda pop, cigarettes, a boombox, and bikinis. If you were lucky to get time alone with the missus at the beach, you frolicked in the water, bodies favorably close, and possibly took a walk, napped, or did anything, without kids bothering you, in quick peace. Then after the beach you ended up somewhere with immediate access to margaritas or cold beer and chicken wings.

Your dad beach duty starts now

A beach day with the kids means at least two hours prep at home dressing the kids and packing. Then there's the drive. Then there's filling up the Beach Buddy Buggy with cooler, chairs, blankets, towels, shovels, pails, and the like, and then dragging it a quarter of a mile to a spot of Earth that the sun will bear down on all day (oh you thought wheels on your Beach Buddy Buggy were helpful? Fool!). You then have to dig holes for the umbrellas and/or build a tent while setting up camp. Oh, yes. The beach is like camping except that when you are camping (or having a picnic), you don't always have to worry about something falling in the grass because we all know the five second rule, and grass always seems kind of clean. But not sand. Not that cursed, desert material that rules the beach.

But while at the beach, dear readers, you're in the blazing hot sun, half naked, setting up a complicated array of chairs and blankets while the kids bug you to just go in the water already daddy, guarding your food and perspiring water bottle away from the Earth because sand gets in and on everything. I don't mind sandy feet or a little sand at home from the kids' bathing suits, but this invasive alien crawls into every space, wrinkle, and available niche it can. And please, oh please let the kids already have sunscreen on, because lathering up children on the hot sand is the very last thing anyone wants to do, especially when they're already sandy from the 4.2 minutes you've actually been at the beach.

In the real world we seek shade, proper covering, and air conditioning – but not on a beach day. In the real world we never dig up the backyard to make dirt castles – but not on a beach day. In the real world we hope for peace after death in a nice, cool, cloudy heaven- but not on a beach day. In the real world, we dress professionally or at least we cover up most of our skin – but not on a beach day. The beach allows us to be lazy savages in the hot, deadly sun.

There are only so many things to do at the beach, so you have to be inventive because you'll be there longer than you want but just long enough so that the missus feels like it was a "long beach day." So just get used to not checking the time. Don't be like that, dad.

Okay we climbed the rocks, check. We swam around, check. Caught hermit crabs, regular crabs, and tadpoles, check. Took a walk, check. Tried to nap, check. Ate kids' leftover lunch when they were not looking, check. Bought overpriced ice cream and goods from the beach restaurant or truck, check. Tried checking your smartphone for a distraction, check. Tried reading a book, check. Built a sandcastle or something like it, check. Tried to people-watch, check. Checked checkered skin for sunburn check-marks, check. Time gone by: forty-three minutes.

Cold beer, warm skin

So, dear men, if you can hold out long enough, however, then driving home with your ocean-kissed skin adjusting in the shade of the car will make it all worthwhile. You don't even care that you're wearing slightly dried, slightly wet shorts. The trunk is sufficiently filled with sand – ain't no thang. You'll be dead tired and dehydrated at work tomorrow–who cares. Your pasty white skin is red but the wife looks great (that sunbathing makes her all the more delicious).

So it's all good because the wife is happy and the kids are exhausted, and you get to drink cold beer at home and watch some TV. You'll do anything to get to this place because you are a man, and a dad, and alive in the summer.

The "Ready to Die But Still Alive" Suicide Club (and the Life That Follows)

"I know, too, that death is the only god who comes when you call." (Roger Zelazny, Frost & Fire)

SINCE A YOUNG AGE I've thought about death, dying, or suicide almost every day—through adolescence when I had my depressive and "serious consideration of self-terminus" bouts, into adulthood where anxiety and despair claimed my quieter hours, and into my 30s where the drudgery and angst of life are just daily coats I hang up because I've been alive enough to know about better days, true joy, and the long life of adventure waiting for us.

But let's be real about the lifers who experience depression and suicidal thoughts for years on end, past those awful teenage years when impulsive actions claim many, and into life after marriage, kids, career, and any post-college enlightenment.

You see, I have a full, wonderful life, but *it* has always been there, like a grey friend waiting with me, patiently, sometimes giving me strength in those "just let go" moments, when I'm reminded that there is no center to the universe, that failure is okay, and that life always goes on—and feeling this certain way actually saves me a little.

Life goes on—always. With or without you. It's this bleak point of view that is refreshing, that I get to live another day because I've decided to live another day, and that whatever life will throw at me, I've already been down so long I can't help but remind our *friend—the "it"*—that I've already considered it all, and I'm okay with living.

Because life with me alive is better for everyone, even though some of us know that at the lowest points of depression and suicidal thinking erase those guilty, blessed feelings.

It's sort of a lifelong "ready to die" feeling rather than a "want to die" emotion that we should all be talking about.

And on World Suicide Prevention Day, it was wonderful to see all of these encouraging memes and statements on Facebook and Twitter, but I know that they won't all work.

And they *shouldn't* work, because they *can't* always work (and they don't). Some things—a day of awareness, a friend's consolation, an intervention—just can't work long-term for those with persistent, chronic, major, or manic depression, or for those who live with PTSD, grief, ennui, melancholy, or just good old fashioned existential angst.

It's always there, inside your chest, lying to others, and waiting its turn.

It's just like that.

But that doesn't mean there isn't hope for those who are currently or frequently suicidal, or that encouragement won't work on those who are in the throes of an episode that will lead to suicide.

I just know that for me, it wouldn't have worked during previous dark times when suicide was on my mind like anything else—variations of the how-to (scenarios that seemed inevitable) and periods of deep longing for an end, even though everything seemed normal, healthy, and ordinary.

But, for those who have dealt with depression and suicidal thoughts since they were young, there is a secret niche that we don't talk about, burrowed in the years of wood and stone: it *doesn't* always get better—it just gets *quieter*.

Most of the time.

Let's be real about suicidal feelings.

I'm not going to describe in detail my own suicide attempts or share with you the times when I helped and reached out to those who were depressed and/or suicidal, nor am I going to share the stories of those who I've known who are no longer with us.

But I will share the *inverse* of my saving grace from back in the day when it seemed inevitable that I would kill myself, which is:

Just wait until tomorrow.

Like a neatly crocheted wall hanging, I convinced myself that "Kill Yourself Tomorrow" would be my daily affirmation until I didn't need it anymore.

If life felt so awful, I told myself, then let life be a slow death.

And eventually, I stopped being suicidal and learned to live with those feelings, which changed into a livable melancholy that I wear, and that changes as I get older.

Almost twenty years ago, there weren't any anti-suicide campaigns, days, or messages the way we have it today, and to be honest, if there had been one, I would have—like many depressive and suicidal people—ignored it because, depending on the level of depression, no one but me could pull me out.

And I pulled myself out.

That is, over time—a long time, that is—I pulled myself out, with the help of close friends, from my late teens on toward and through adulthood.

Let's be real about this—is it okay for us to want to die, even for a spell?
No amount of semicolon tattoos on wrists, "it gets better" messages, or encouraging proverbs would have worked.

Religion, friends and family intervention, literature, romantic relationships, and distractions didn't subside the feelings or make them go away.

And as I get older I realize that some of us just get *stuck* with these feelings of dread and melancholy, and you have to find a way to live with it.

And when someone *does* take their life, it kind of makes sense in the worst, most obvious way.

Eventually, in the arc of my mature life, I became too old for suicide—even though that's a silly assumption—but as a father, I wouldn't want to miss out on a life with my children and wife, or a chance to grow old, or a chance to slow life so that maybe *it* would finally leave without any trace.

At a younger age, I knew it all—or I thought I did: I was valuable to people around me and, of course, they would be affected if I had taken my life—but it wasn't about them. It was about me. Plus, when you're dead, you don't feel guilt for dying. But you do leave a mess of trauma, pain, hate, guilt, and depression for those who never were depressed in the first place.

"Do something?" There's nothing you can do. For some cases. There really isn't. We smile on #PreventionDay and then it's back to a life-long conversation with *our friend.*

Some would call this cynical, but I think I'm being realistic.

Maybe this is why such a big killer of men and women gets such little notice, because we don't want it to be there, undoing us, highlighting what is perceived as weakness when it's not cowardice at all.

And adults on the whole won't address it possibly because—government intervention or otherwise—of the fear of being weak, or the hesitation that if we give it a name we'll have to confront this totally normal *I want to die* attitude in society.

Imagine a *war on feeling shitty.*

In the end

Although I had close, sympathetic friends who were there for me during many dark times, and some who were compassionate (and those who had no idea or those who did and didn't know what to do), in the end, it was me alone forcing myself to get over it and stay alive for the next season of life. Then a season more. Then a season more. I decided to give myself life rather than take it.

So—I want to live, and live deep.

I want to grieve.

I want to endure those feelings of suffering (or not), and experience every moment of my life, whether it be full of dread, anxiety, or other.

It is a wonderful life. That is, all the wonderful parts of it.

And you and I have the power to stay alive, for one more day, and then another—and then another—to meet us on the other side of several decades from its start.

I'll see you there.

How to Protest Properly and Be a Young Dad at the Same Time

BACK IN MY ACTIVIST and rock and roll days, I had a moment to define whatever movement I feel like I'm a part of for life: I was standing next to Noam Chomsky at T.T. the Bear's in Boston listening to Howard Zinn speak. Let me write that again—I was standing next to Noam Chomsky while watching Howard Zinn speak.

If you live in Boston, there are a few times this kind of thing might happen. If you don't live in Boston, or the Northeast, or aren't part of the kind of crowd that reveres or seeks out this kind of thing, it was a big deal that happened by accident, but still happened.

It was one of those moments I'll forever hold in that weird celebrity part of my brain, like when I sat next to John Updike in a movie theatre (well, across the aisle) or talking with then Senator Kerry while waiting for my turn on the microphone at an AFL-CIO conference, or getting a half an hour with Kurt Vonnegut Jr. in his office when he was teaching at Smith College.

I'm enough distanced from these moments that now when I think of them, I do so as a Dad. When you're young you march and protest alongside other young people, and then you go out to celebrate and publish the happenings in your 'zine. Then you pick it up again as soon as you can, and repeat. When you're a little older and a parent, you march and protest as long as there's a sitter, or you can do so around preschool hours and days off.

The Movement is always moving, however old you're getting.

On this MLK day, I think of Dr. King the Dad, recalling his constant referencing to his children over the course of his life as a speaker and essayist. Like him, all parents have a grandiose view of an idyllic society, one where our kids can play and learn in peace. As a parent, continual maintenance of the local playground is more of a focal point for city activism than fighting the WTO or corporations or the Man.

This is where true change happens in a society: moms and dads making it nice for everyone. And this sentiment is essentially the idea behind every great movement: let's just make it nice for everyone.

You know, for the kids.

Since Dr. King's day, the marches and sit-ins have changed dramatically in focus—in a First World setting, we're fighting for things like Minimum Wage increase, the Dream Act, Sustainability, Marriage Equality, and some equitable legislation toward solving the drop-out rate in high schools while fighting the effects of poverty seen in American children (and hopefully children around the world).

We're signing petitions online between play dates and diaper changes, and posting the you-should-care-about-this videos and memes on social media while getting ready for that second job so the kids can have a few more presents during the holidays. Aside from a pro-breastfeeding "sit-in" and Farmer's Market signature collecting, parents don't have the same marching and parade options as the parents in the 60s and 70s did, although the Unions keep this proud tradition alive, and every now and then we'll see millions gathered for a cause (gee, I'd really like to Occupy Boston, but I have to work and take the kids to soccer). But while we're fighting for the reparations of the last list of incongruities here in the First World, there is a huge world of Dads and Moms out there just trying to make ends meet in countries where food and vaccines can't just be bought at the other CVS or Walgreens in your city.

The other day I was pleased to hear my kindergartener tell me about an outdated world where there were "Whites Only" signs and people were mean to each other because of skin color. We talked about being kind, peaceful, and how to share, and what Dr. King did to help people. Absent from the conversation was the heavy topic of racism, but for a six year old in today's world, ideas about race from the 1960s can be summed up in that wonderful story of:

Once Upon A Time people were mean to each other because of skin color, and now they're not as mean.
And that's pretty much it, from Dad to Child: you just have to be kind and fair. My four year old constantly asks why we look white and pink (why do people look like each other? is one of my favorite questions from her), and I tell her about DNA and families and somehow she gets it (although she thinks all females have brown eyes and all males have blue eyes, which is only because she and her mother have brown eyes while the boy and I have blue).

To add to this, we live in a drastically different media world than ever before, as if Handy Manny, Dora, and Doc McStuffins have led the way for our children to see the world in a way that I only started to see back in the 80s. Is this the romantic future the marchers were imagining back in the abolition days and on through towards the 60s? Maybe so.

And so, on this MLK Day, I salute the thirty-something Dad who spoke, marched, petitioned, protested, was jailed for, and preached on behalf of his children, their classmates and their families, and how he continues to inspire this thirty-something Dad to speak out and write on behalf of my children and their classmates and their families when and where I can, albeit in a different world than it was a few generations ago, and toward the (brand) new or revised world it will be by the time my children are writing about their children.

Because after all is done and said, and the hashtags and signs are put away, it's all about—and for—the kids. Dr. King knew and preached that, and we should never stop doing so, wherever we're standing and watching, marching and singing, or simply raising our children to be helpful, loving, and kind.

Why I'm Running for President (and Why You Should Too)

THANK THE FOUNDING FATHERS and Mothers for a long American campaign season. This gives the people and media enough time to fall in love with, cover, and analyze and then forget the very people who think they're qualified enough to lead the free world.

And I'm one of them.

Well, not really. But let me explain.

The Dream Starts
In short—I'm now, at 36-years-old and American-born, qualified, according to the Constitution, to run. It also happens to be a perfect year for a "young" candidate like me to run and make waves, hopefully inspiring others and achieving a life-long dream. Since I sang for President Clinton's first Inauguration when I was an eighth grader, I had this feeling—like many people my age, and many individuals who have taken part in grandiose events like a young President Clinton meeting Kennedy—that I could be the one to change the world, to be a leader, to be, say, the president. That feeling has changed since some twenty years ago, but somewhere along the way, from teenage-hood to parenthood, I became stuck with this dream of running for president.

It's too late for me to quickly earn my doctorate, law degree, or have a quick political rise from local elected leader to national figure, so I'm well aware of my limitations. At best I'm a gum-chewing English teacher with big ideas and a sense of humor, and yet I still want to run (secretly I know I could really do it, even with the long hours).

So, realizing that I probably won't win, at least I *can* run. When I'm old, I can look back and say that I once ran for President. I'll have that story.

This is about Your Dream

Of all the passions I've had in life, I've been able to come to terms that some of them just can't happen right now, but I can't go through life knowing that I've given up on some of them. I put several dreams on hold (for good reasons) while cultivating my career as a teacher and now as a writer. My life as a husband and father more than gives me the greatest sense of purpose and center. I realize that some dreams can happen later, much later, and some have to happen right now, while the irons are hot. Some things—school, babies, falling in love—happen when they happen, and just end up right. Some don't.

But some things—a business, a home, a relationship, finishing school, or mending a broken friendship—need to be done right here, right now. Years from now the time will have passed and the waters will have run dry. And you never know the why or how, except that the time was, and you didn't take action.

2016 happens to be that time for me. Maybe—just maybe—it's the same time for you.

McKeen the Dream in 2016

It's as if my campaign slogan was written in the pun-tastic stars. My last name and "dream" and "teen" rhyme (or near rhyme). And this won't happen again, ever. Especially while I'm young.

But actually my heritage and professional life have somewhat prepared me for this kind of thinking. My ancestor and signer of the Declaration of Independence, Thomas McKean, was one of the early Presidents of the Continental Congress, who were predecessors to the role of the now

President of the U.S.A. Some historians say that they were the original presidents of the United States. Huh.

I've also had a small political career as a Union representative (for which I'm extremely proud) and a term serving as a Futures Union Representative—the first one—for the M.A. AFL-CIO. I was able to share stages with presidents, senators, and governors, all because I decided to run for the position, even though I didn't know if I was qualified. But I was willing to speak, work, and show up, and I was able to make valuable connections with masters of their trades, executives, and the amazing staff personnel behind them.

But that's where the trail runs dry. I've spent my professional life as a teacher, coach, and writer, and that's the experience I bring to the table. As an only child of teachers and an educator myself, I've seen how Americans live and dream. And I'm living the dream myself: I'm happy and love what I do and the family I come home to each night. At the same time I realize how many other versions of life are just as normal, and how much need there is from every home and body, regardless of station or education.

There is nothing in your "fate," however, that can achieve success for you. Being born doesn't make you any one thing in life, and each career path and risky professional choice I've made has been because I've wanted to be able to look back and say, for a while, *I did that*. I *was that*. I had a time of it. And I was good at it.

If I was President

So here it is—my year to gear up and run. It will be part experiment, part entertainment, and a complete experience from which to draw. I aim at least to get on the ballot in my state and to say, after a bit of hard work, that I ran. Who knows what could happen?

And, more importantly, the same goes for you out there making that decision for the most important season of your life—the business may fail, the creation may not last, the relationship might go south, the band might break up—but you didn't say no at the right time, and that's what you can talk about when you remember the better parts of the thing that failed.

So do something big, unexpected, crazy—something you've been dreaming about, even if it's foolish. You never know what positive things may come.

This is my year (or the year leading up to it). Yours too.

Let's get started.

Because, Gentlemen -- Last Thoughts on Rape Culture

GENTLEMEN AND LADIES OF THE WORLD, it's time to be brutally honest about sexual assault and rape culture.

And when I write "gentlemen" (and for many women who are just as guilty), I mean *all* men, because many of you aren't gentle in words or deeds even though you're convinced you are.

Because our culture is obsessed with sex and sexualizing women from a young age and on throughout and until death—

Because our culture (and most cultures) is a "rape culture," filled with discriminatory and unattainable standards of beauty, and constantly blaming women for unwanted sexual advances and rape—

Because we allow catcalling, physical and verbal abuse, and sexual assault against our women (and yes, men) from a pre-pubescent age to adulthood—

Because "cute," "pretty," "princess-like," and "beautiful" are the go-to adjectives and states of assumed being for our girls, young women, and daughters who aren't old enough to know what "sexualized" means, I have the following:

It needs to stop. Now.

Women don't and never deserve rape, unwarranted attention, sexual assault, catcalling, or any variety of these typical cultural standards that have been with us as humans since the very beginning.

Only consensual sex will do; only non-sexual compliments will suffice; only the most respectful comments for our daughters, sisters, and mothers will stand.

So I will offer the following advice in a series of he thought/he said in hopes that we can start fresh with the reader—from the mind of a man who reasons rape culture away, and from the justifications of cultures around the world (and most recently from media coverage of First World election-heavy-America).

Please apply all that apply:

Women love the attention, so therefore it's okay to catcall and aggressively compliment them on their appearance.

No, it's not okay.

Not even if the lady says thank you?

No.

Not even if the lady wears skin-revealing clothing and is showing off her body? Don't they *want* a compliment?

Not even then. Even if they like being told nice things, which everyone does. Everyone wants compliments in life, especially when they dress up. People do it every day.

Okay, I get "aggressively compliment" but what about just a nice statement about their legs, breasts, butt, face, or arms?

No, especially no. Just because you're attracted to "beautiful things" doesn't mean you get to comment on them, as much as you want to reach out and touch, kiss, hold, fondle, grope, or have sex with them. You have to fight this every day. Just because you want and think you are entitled to something—anything, and especially human beings—means nothing if it's not reciprocal.

What if they deserve it?

This is part of the problem—you thinking that women "deserve" the compliment—and that they want more than a compliment to follow—that they are on display just for you.

Of course they are on display! A compliment is just a compliment—nothing more.

From a young age, women are complimented as a way of putting them in their "place" as the beauty and sex-bearers of our culture. Most men and women do this all the time and don't think twice about it—ever. Then the girls are pressured from that young age to be attractive and sexy no matter what. We do the same to boys with equally disturbing standards.

Look, women like compliments, and if they're going to dress sexily, then I'm going to treat them like they want to be treated, even if that means shouting out a compliment from across the street—not that I do it, but I get it.

Even to 10 year-olds?

No, that's too young, of course.

13 year-olds?

Come on with that.

15 year-olds? Most women have heard sexual compliments and been talked to this way—and worse—from younger than ten years old.

Listen, you make all men sound like pervs and rapists. Men *like* looking at women, and women who dress a certain way (I hate to say it) *deserve* it—especially if they're leading someone on. They're showing off their bodies, so it's their fault when men advance. We can't help it!

And therein lies the problem. We can help it. We should help it. When men leer and stare, they're not just being rude and pervy, but they're conditioning one more woman to put up with it. There has to be a stop.

I don't have to listen to this. Women are just as sexual as men are, and none of us can help it. And every now and then, women really are "asking for it" even though you think they're just dressing up for themselves or their girlfriends.

And therein lies the problem, again. The heart of the "compliment" and catcalling is often a means to sexual assessment, which leads to a justification on a spectrum of sexual assault.

Well look, men would love to be catcalled and sexually harassed.

And raped?

No, now you're taking it too far.

Not when 90 percent of rape cases are women who were raped. And when women bear a lifetime of catcalling, compliment, and sexual assault, rape culture continues. It has been said that 90% of rapes go unreported. We have a problem, and the problem starts here.

And no—men who realize that women bear the brunt of catcalling, sexual assault, groping, and rape worldwide and from a young age would want that for themselves.

And we shouldn't want that for them either.

Every kid wants to be complimented.

Every kid wants to please adults.

Every person wants to dress how they feel they best look to the world—whether showing off certain body parts is alluring to someone else or not.

Every person should have a right to "feel sexy" or confident or proud about their body without harmful, traumatic, and unwanted solicitation from anyone else.

And they shouldn't have to live in fear or sexual dismissal or appraisal at any age, no matter what.

Every adult and near-adult person is a sexual creature who deserves consensual sex that is healthy for both parties.

Yes, men have evolved differently than women.

Yes, on the whole, men are "visually stimulated" more so than women.

Yes, men have a strong desire to own beauty and control the things they want and think they need—include any and all justifications of sexual action and assault.

But we have to do better—better for our culture, our women, our daughters, our boys, and ourselves.

No one deserves to be groped, molested, assaulted, or raped against their will—including men and boys—for any reason.

Ever.

Even if the woman or man wants sex and changes her or his mind.

Even if the couple has a sexual history.

Even if things started out consensual and stopped midway through.

Even if our sex-obsessed culture seems to demand it.

Even if your family and friends demand or excuse it.

Even if presidents, senators, congressmen, preachers, voters, and men and women with loud and powerful voices demand it.

Even now, since forever, and until the last children of the last generation are ushered into adulthood with a healthy sense of their bodies.

Even though it's taken us this long to get to this place of understanding.

The Luxury of Two Beers at the End of the Day

MY NEEDS ARE SIMPLE: a hearty tax shelter, healthy pension, robust health insurance, generous sick days, fully stocked fridge, a little extra cash after paying the rent, and seven beers, preferably craft or imported.

My tastes are sort of set in their ways.

That, and—of course—perfect health for my wife and kids, is all I need, on top of the basics of modern First World living. Forget a new house, car, clothes, and forget Paris. Give me the know-how of there being enough beer in the fridge for the end of a long day of hard work where I've earned every dollar. I want to hear that clink-clink when the fridge door is open.

I'm not asking to *drink* seven beers a night, but I want the financial freedom to enjoy one or two if I want, and to have seven more in the fridge waiting for me, for tomorrow or the weekend. I want the ability to drink or share with the wife or friends—it might be a Bourbon and ginger ale, or a gin and tonic, but the principle remains. I want that bordering-hoarder pleasure of having luxury in reserve, when I want.

I want that financial freedom.

And eventually I'll have it. Maybe when the kids are out of college. I don't want to die on my feet, a sweaty worker who didn't know how to be smart about money, especially in my American lower-middle-class world, where I've been privileged enough to reach a point and skill set that can guide me towards a retirement and help me provide for my children until they can provide for themselves.

What is a dollar?

Let's talk about $7—specifically the amount (give or take sixty cents) it costs to afford seven beers or seven burgers or seven of something in your refrigerator. That seven dollars is swallowed up by the big picture—the cost of the fridge, electricity, the contents within—plus the pantry and its accoutrements. That $7 is a small slice of rent or a mortgage, or of a movie ticket or water bill. You know what things cost. The cost of take-out versus a week of groceries, the price of beer and coffee versus milk, and the cost of luxury, however simple, versus holding out until you really deserve that luxurious finish, whatever it may be.

When times are tight, the luxuries go, and you start that mental list: seven dollars here, seven dollars there. Eventually you start peeling back the years to your first dollar, wishing you had saved every nickel spent on any luxury since you first started working, just so you could have that luxury *now*. Rent? That'll be 1,500 beers. That new Lego set or dance lessons for junior? 40 to 60 beers. Interestingly enough, the Department of Agriculture recently raised their cost of raising a child to 304,000 beers from conception to college move-in. And forget buying a round of frosty ones at the bar—that ends up being like 30 beers to pay for, well, roughly seven beers.

The rent—and everything else—is just too damn high!

Most of the world lives on less than $2 a day. You've heard that, I'm sure—probably so much so that you can't imagine what it looks like, or you can see it in your mind's eye or on TV and you just don't know what to do about it (you could start learning here on TED, actually).

What we need is a level playing field, which is something that has never existed in history. The top percentile have always owned the majority of everything, and the rest of us have always scrambled like morons for what was left, whether it was real estate or the last Christmas toy your kid wanted more than anything else (which happened to cost 63 beers, but was worth it).

The freedom, however, is in the refusal to be anxious about the money. Everything has always been insanely expensive, it seems—from shoes for kindergarten and large textbooks for college to that extra stupid polo the restaurant wants you to purchase (trust me, you'll want it). And you probably already know that there doesn't have to be any beer in the fridge or extra meat for the grill. Some of us know how to *go without* better than others, and some of us never have to.

Eventually everyone has their own object-to-money-connector. For me it's beer or take-out or tattoos. For you it may be shirts or shovels or wainscoting. We're all just out here looking to get something to eat, right?

Jack of all trades, Master of English

It turns out the world has enough writers and English professors, and also enough landscapers and house painters. But it can always use one more—that's where I come in, as do legions of teachers in the summer. Those of you with degrees know the pressure of paying off your debts when you might not have the right job or career (yet) to show for it—or the pressure of paying off your college debt when you never finished.

My saving grace is that I've never turned down a half-interesting job where I could either learn something new or be able to have an adventure while making enough money for the usual reasons. And I've had a lot of jobs, both within my career and without. Some jobs have led to long-lasting wells and some were means to an end. Some provided enough for the landlord and tax-man, and some left the beer drawer empty for weeks. Today, however, I'm able to be proud of my motley resume, and I can call up experiences some bosses didn't know I had (or didn't need to know). The day I'm not hungry to work and learn will be the day that I am either a little too old for risk and adventure, or the day that I finally have done enough to write full time about it all. Either way, I'm never retiring. I just couldn't.

All you need is love—and a nest egg
Back to my "simple" needs: obviously, and I want to make this clear—if you have a good work ethic, healthy relationships, and general happiness, you're already rich beyond any means. You really are. If you're stressed about "making it," you're not alone: most people *aren't* making or saving enough money to live comfortably, even week to week, from high school teachers to hedge fund managers. Hopefully you have loved ones to fart around with on the couch after a long day; hopefully you have a pension free from the grubby hands of future workers and governments; hopefully you have ice cream and beer in the fridge for when the kids go to bed.

Now who's buying?

I Just Want the Old, Good Days of Parenting— Before the Nest Was Empty

I DON'T WANT TO MULCH THIS SATURDAY.
I know it's our big to-do for when the weather's right, but I don't want to. I want to do things young people with kids do, like a soccer game or dance recital or gymnastics. Like the old days. Like the good old days. Remember when the kids were young—too young to be saying things like "I kind of miss the old, good days"—but they would always say that, exactly like that, unaware of how short their lives had been at that moment?

But we're old. I'd kill to be twenty-five again, or thirty-five, or even fifty-five. Definitely not fifteen. I don't have the energy for that. Everything went so fast. Our last kid is already twenty-five and out of the house and now we finally have all the rooms to ourselves. Sonny is the age we were when he was born—Junior is right behind, and the Baby is on her own, now, still the baby. The railing in the old house is finally steady, the mornings couldn't be quieter, the cars are paid off. We finally have our twenties back, before kids, more or less—more here, much less there.

Not that we're sad old sacks. We're not. We're the children of the children of the Greatest Generation. But none of that matters. I just want more time when the kids were young, even the last of their teenage years, when they didn't want us as much. Even the college years when we rarely saw them. How ever did we go days without talking? How did they become their own people? I guess they were born that way, really. But they grew, and grew.

They were so young just a minute ago, and then—
I want to pick them up from preschool, and high school, and college for that first time—or last time.

I want to comfort one of them after an adolescent break-up or hold them after a serious fall; I want to cuddle on the couch—remember when they wanted to cuddle all the time?

I want to watch them struggle with their homework and those first jobs and then the real first jobs.

I want snow days and birthdays and those first few days of summer—hell, any day of any summer at the beach.

I want to relive the moments after that first serious E.R. visit, when we realized it would be all right, and the times when we didn't know which way it would go. And the fights—between the kids and between the kids and us, even those I want to live through, one more time.

I would settle just to be on the same floor with them, listening to them play in the next room, one last time. I wouldn't have to interact with them. I just love listening to them.

Any moment where they held my hand or looked me in the eye without any pretense or fear or question—or any time I knew they had to count on me to wake them up or dress them or get them somewhere on time. They still give me those young looks sometimes, and hopefully I still have those eyes they first stared at when they couldn't walk and we would just hold them all the time. They used to use my eyes and face to learn how to react to the world.

Our life was—it still is—like a really good TV show that I more than love, and I just want it back, you know, to watch again, all the episodes, especially the children's episodes—there were so many of them. I couldn't get enough of them when they were happening. And we took so many pictures.

And the grandchildren. Oh, the new joys—but they're no Sonny or Junior or the Baby. At least not like it was. All those firsts—they're not ours to have. Not like the old, good days.

But mulching is good. Mulching is necessary. It's one of those things we do. We're not getting any younger, we never were. It felt like we were when the kids were young, and then at one point we were older, and then older still, and then we weren't the young parents in the pictures anymore.

But that's okay. We have our life—our long, incredible life—together, with kids. We have more than we planned for, and more to come. We built this world, somehow, and filled it with everything we could, and then it just kept going. And to think we were young and in love just a few pictures and memories and decades ago.

And if I'm quiet, I can hear the past, outside a door somewhere, or up the stairs—I'm listening in for a moment that belongs only to me, preserved in a place some time ago, somewhere circling my veins in cells I still feel like I did when we were young.

References

Allen, Woody, director. *Deconstructing Harry*. Fine Line Features, 1997.

Building Something Out of Nothing. *Modest Mouse*. Up Records, 1999.

Fitzgerald, F S. *The Great Gatsby*. New York: Scribner Paperback Fiction, 1995.

Imagine. *John Lennon*. Apple Records, 1971.

Shakespeare, William. Mowat, Barbara A. Werstine, Paul. *The Tragedy Of Macbeth*. New York : Washington Square Press, 2004, c1992.

Zelazny, Roger. *Frost and Fire*. Avon Books, 1989.

CPSIA information can be obtained
at www.ICGtesting.com
Printed in the USA
LVHW010054230620
658655LV00006B/973